D0454890

A DIFFERENT ANGLE

FLY FISHING STORIES BY WOMEN

EDITED BY HOLLY MORRIS

SEAL PRESS

Cover photograph by Harley Soltes
Polaroid transfer by Anne Hillam
Interior art by Michael DalCerro
Cover and book design by Clare Conrad

Acknowledgments:
"Blood Knots," by Mallory Burton, was originally published in *Flyfisher* magazine, Winter 1990. "The Company of Men," by Pam Houston, was originally published in *Elle* magazine, September 1993. "Love the Man, Love the Fly Rod," by Allison Moir, was originally published in slightly different form in *Forbes FYI*, May 10, 1993. "The Island" from *Little Rivers: Tales of a Woman Angler* by Margot Page. Copyright © 1995 by Margot Page. Reprinted by permission of Lyons & Burford Publishers. "Somewhere with Sven," by E. Annie Proulx was originally published as "You Know You've Been Somewhere When You've Been Somewhere With Sven" in *Outside* magazine, December 1993. "Midstream" excerpted from *Midstream: The Story of a Mother's Death and a Daughter's Renewal* by Le Anne Schreiber. Copyright © 1990 by Le Anne Schreiber. Reprinted by permission of Viking Publishers. "A Fly Fishing Life" excerpted from *Joan Wulff's Fly Fishing* by Joan Wulff. Copyright © 1991 by Joan Wulff. Reprinted by permission of Stackpole Books.

Library of Congress Cataloging-in-Publication Data
A different angle : fly fishing stories by women / edited by Holly Morris.
ISBN 1-878067-63-X (hardcover)
1. Fly fishing. 2. Women fishers. I. Morris, Holly, 1965–
SH456.D55   1995   799.1'2—dc20   94-39386

Printed in the United States of America
First printing, April 1995
10 9 8 7 6 5 4 3 2 1

Distributed to the trade by Publishers Group West
In Canada: Publishers Group West Canada, Toronto, Ontario
In the U.K. and Europe: Airlift Book Company, London, England

Acknowledgements

During the time this book was in progress, numerous people gave generously of their support, advice and professional skills. Special thanks to Michael DalCerro, Anne Hillam, Nick Lyons, Jeannie Morris, Laura Slevin, Harley Soltes and Elizabeth Wales for their varied contributions.

I am grateful for the infinite patience and skills of the women of Seal Press. My exceptional editor Faith Conlon once again demonstrated her many gifts of intelligence and insight, as well as her valuable friendship; Cathy Johnson worked wonders with her skilled copyeditor's hand; art director Clare Conrad created this beautiful edition and provided a remarkable camaraderie; production manager Stacy M. Lewis, who often went above and beyond the call of duty, used a keen mind and unflagging diligence to organize a sometimes chaotic manuscript into a final book. I also thank Emily Arfin, Ingrid Emerick, Rebecca Engrav, Lynn Siniscalchi, June Thomas and Barbara Wilson for their efforts and enthusiasm toward this collection.

Thanks also to the many women whose writing was submitted for publication but could not be included.

Finally, for their hard work, endlessly good spirits and many talents, I thank the writers who created *A Different Angle*. It has been a great pleasure to work with and come to know this very special group of women whose words add a new chapter to the sport and literature of fly fishing.

In memory of Jeanne Dutro Hatteberg

and

For John Hatteberg

CONTENTS

Introduction

The world of sport offers flashes of brilliance that linger in our mind: the grace of a seamless turn at second for the double play, the airborne energy of a Jordanesque slam dunk, the daring precision of a soaring triple axle. These moments of perfection transcend the contest, carrying us beyond sweat, muscle and competition to a higher plane where physical effort becomes artistry.

Fly fishing offers the potential to find such moments in endless, ever-changing ways. Perhaps it is the flash of a strike, the elegance of a release, or the simple satisfaction of watching an unfurling arc of line. Fly fishing moments are often solitary and fleeting, but they are deeply and sometimes inexplicably compelling. Those who survive the trials of the neophyte—fatal casts, sodden waders and fishless days—to become fluent in the muted colors and dignified prose of fly fishing, know the magic it can work: a soul scrubbed clean of life's trivia, the experience of witnessing nature's subtle rhythms, the possibility of a perfect day.

At its best, fly fishing brings the gifts of grace and clarity that Virginia Woolf called "moments of being," those privileged moments when a personal or cosmic truth is perceived in a flash of intuition. Such moments fuel the desire to express fly fishing's essence through another solitary and creative endeavor— the act of writing. The sport's unique blend of the physical and the meditative has inspired an enormous and rich body of literature. But catching the seductive qualities of fly fishing on the page can prove as elusive as charming a wily brook trout out of its lie. As with a faint star in the night's sky, one can better understand fishing's allure by looking around it, off to the side, not right at it.

The beguiling draw that has us wetting a line at every opportunity and armchair angling through long winter months has a power that transcends gender and culture. Yet despite the intrinsic appeal and rewards of fly fishing, not to mention its lack of dependence on brawn and bravura, it is a sport that until recently has been defined by a certain tradition and a specific gender. For centuries, men, not women, have been handed the rods and reels and taught the finesse of a flawless presentation and the secrets of matching the hatch. Men have been schooled to the beat of the metronome. Men have written about wading into pristine waters in search of a swatch of silver from another world. Blame it on women's limited access to leisure time and wealth, impenetrable traditions or gender roles; whatever the reason, women have not been a visible part of the fly fishing world, nor its literature.

Women's absence from the tradition is ironic when one considers the colorful figure of Dame Juliana Berners, a nun and noblewoman who is credited with writing the first fly fishing essay, *The Treatise of Fishing with an Angle* (circa 1421). In addition to offering sage advice about how and when to fish, Dame Juliana's praise sounded a chord that was to be echoed for centuries: "The sport and game of angling is the true means and cause that brings a man (*sic*) into a merry spirit, which makes a flowering age and a long one." In light of Dame Juliana's pioneering fishing wisdom, it is astonishing that it has taken nearly six centuries for women to have a book of fly fishing stories to call their own.

Today, the face of fly fishing is changing. Women are enjoying the sport in unprecedented numbers, reinterpreting its traditions and creating some of their own. A handful of anglers in the last two centuries have led the way—Cornelia Crosby blazed a trail for female outdoor journalists with her column "Fly Rod's Notebook"; Mary Orvis Marbury, author of *Favorite Flies and*

Their Histories (1892), helped build fly fishing's best known company; Sara J. McBride, Carrie Stevens and Helen Shaw all became masters in the art of fly tying—yet for the most part, women's entry into the sport has been an adventure in un-mapped territory. But as this century comes to a close, women are adding their voices to the lexicon of fly fishing and writing themselves into the literature.

A Different Angle presents writing from a new perspective, a female perspective, one that offers a satisfying blend of surprise, drama, renewal, humor and insight. Whether it is a perceptive look at midstream machismo or a new reverence for the wildness of the natural world, each story reflects the fresh ideas and many dimensions women are bringing to the sport.

As they do in other aspects of their lives, women approach fly fishing holistically, weaving the fabric of their lives and rela-tionships into their fishing. Great gonzo stories laced with com-petition and one-upmanship are not the norm. Here you'll find an irreverent story of an all-women group of anglers who un-cover the power of estrogen while floating down the Des-chutes—a story that not only celebrates fishing as a shared event but also offers a new twist on the theme of fly fishing through midlife.

Several of the writers in this collection fish with spouses or male friends as equals—including one who, chest-high in a bone-chilling river at midnight amid a group of poets, tries to discover the essence of male bonding, and another who plunges into fly fishing under the rallying cry "love the man, love the fly rod" and savors the sport long after the man disappears. No longer cardboard fishing widows, the images of women that emerge throughout this book give rise to a new definition of the vener-able "fishing buddy."

Our historical dignitary, Dame Juliana, who was a hunter as well as an angler, professes fly fishing's excellence: "I will now choose among four good sports and honorable pastimes—to wit, among hunting, hawking, fishing and fowling. The best, in my simple judgment, is fishing, called angling, with a rod and a line and a hook." Most of the writers here would agree with Dame Juliana's conclusion that fly fishing is superior to all other "blood sports." What lies at the heart of the traditional "hunt," as well as of most of angling literature, is a search for self. Whereas men are often initiated into fly fishing via the hunt, complete with its rites of passage, solitary quests for self-definition and ambitions to overcome natural forces, women's lack of parallel experiences allows them the freedom to approach the sport from a different direction. The stories here are not laden with age-old rituals of the hunt but have more to do with finding self by moving in tune with nature's rhythms and gently distilling life's many layers. When the hunt has run its course and the fish tally remains unmarked, men and women arrive at a similar, essential place: not a triumph over the natural world but a connection to it and its never-static constellation of mysteries.

Anyone who has watched the grace of a fly fisher casting into a light-dappled pool knows that angling is a sensual exchange with nature. Ask an angler what passed through her mind on a spring-creek morning. "Everything," she might tell you, or perhaps, "It's not just what I was thinking, but what I was feeling, seeing, smelling." Bare in the face of nature's caprice, women come to know themselves in clearer and more basic ways. Life's demands fall away, and a solace, a place to assuage the pain of illness, loss or death is revealed, leaving the spirit refreshed. The possibility of renewal inhabits this collection as surely as rivers meander canyon floors.

But not *all* of these stories plumb the depths of self-discovery or tread waters of spiritual renewal. Just when you're about to take the sport cum art form too seriously, an angler/writer delivers a send-up, a high-spirited bucking of tradition, that will remind you that fishing can be funny, and fun. Being female in a sport dominated by men and seemingly shrouded in esoteric secrets may have its trials, but it does provide good fodder for humor. You'll read how one angler keeps a friendship afloat when waist-deep mud leads to a memorable trip of backcountry chaos. Another wryly fantasizes about homicidal payback for fly fishing clerks—clerks who suddenly materialize when she leaves the rods and reels and crosses the invisible line into the clothing section. A veteran Montana guide confesses "like a person on a talk show" to a singular and momentary fall from grace. (Hint: cheeseballs.) And, of course, you'll discover what is said to be the most significant difference between men and women anglers: Women don't lie about the size.

Poking fun at the zeal fly fishing inspires is not off limits. Most of us who fly fish, or have had the experience of loving a fly fisher, know that once a person is touched by the passion, it can quickly lead to devout—some might say religious—adherence. For those outside the flock, this zealotry is hard to understand: Why brace precariously among slippery rocks in a freezing stream to capture a slimy creature from another world—only to let it go? The parallels between fly fishing and religion are not just literary metaphor: Fly fishing offers the comfort of ritual, harbors a strict code of ethics and inspires a pantheistic philosophy in its devotees. As one woman explains in a satire of her mother's new obsession: "I didn't anticipate the dogma, the intricate litany, the saints, the tithing, the penance. Nor did I anticipate my mother would become the Joan of Arc of fly fishing."

Fish story upon fish story, metaphor upon metaphor, for centuries anglers have written of their passion. The writers in this book are joining fly fishing's public meditation and showing that women are indeed claiming their stretch of the river, creating a new brand of fish story, and contributing to—perhaps changing—a grand and magical literary tradition.

Holly Morris
Seattle, Washington
December 1994

A DIFFERENT ANGLE

LIN SUTHERLAND

A River Ran Over Me

FLY FISHING is beyond sport, skill, and even obsession. It's a religion, and my baptisim into the faith was on the Gunnison River in Colorado. I thought I was merely going to learn something new and different. I didn't anticipate the dogma, the intricate litany, the saints, the tithing, the penance. Nor did I anticipate my mother would become the Joan of Arc of fly fishing.

It started out innocently enough. I chose to take my first stab at fly fishing with Mama because she was a Bass Master of the First Order, the Blood Bait Queen of my youth. But at the age of seventy-two, Mama discovered fly fishing, and as usual, she took something complicated and learned it in about three weeks. Face it, for a woman who took eleven years of Latin in Charleston, South Carolina, anything is easy.

At first she had been skeptical.

"Buncha little snots," she'd remark about fly fishermen. "Effete elitist purists," she'd add.

Then one day she was forced to stop at a little specialty angling shop instead of her usual Live Bait Marina. It was the kind of place that displays fly fishing *ensembles*—and the only reason she went in there was to look for a particular fishing book.

Mama stood there in the front of the store with her calico mane flying and took in the woven creels, leather belts, fifty-dollar floppy fishing hats and six-hundred-dollar graphite rods.

"HEY!" she shouted. "What kind of foo foo fish shop is this?"

Several customers looked around at her and a pony-tailed young man wearing a very expensive fly fishing shirt with a little fly and hook embroidered on its breast pocket rushed forward.

"Yes, Ma'am? May I help you?" he asked.

"Where the hell are your foo foo fish books, young man?" She looked him up and down, then jabbed his chest with one big-knuckled forefinger.

"Young man, you have feathers embroidered on your chest. Just what does that mean?"

He stammered and opened his mouth.

"Nevermind!" she interrupted. "I don't want to know. . . . Hey, here it is—" She reached behind a polished wood counter and pulled out the book she sought.

To make a long story short, Mama and the young man got into a conversation, most of which consisted of her railing about how none of her daughters could fish worth a plugged nickel. The young man turned out to be John Tavenner, a well-respected fly fishing guide from Santa Fe who pulls trout regularly out of the Rio Grande, which hardly anyone could consider a trout stream. He showed my mother boxes of thousands of flies he'd carefully constructed out of chicken necks, hare's ears, and the like. He was twenty-eight but had started fly fishing with his father at the age of twelve.

As happens often to those who meet my mother, Tavenner became intrigued. Mama has a blunt exterior, but you never doubt she's a lady. A Southern lady, at that. Her piercing china-blue eyes shine with intelligence and interest . . . she simply exudes life. The two began to talk fishing, and it wasn't long before Tavenner invited her to attend one of his fly fishing clinics. And that was that. She was the best he'd ever instructed, he told me later. She had the knack.

Working relentlessly, Mama became an expert in about four months, then a total convert. There is nothing worse than a convert, you know, and the next summer she all but forced me to join her and Tavenner at the bottom end of the Black Canyon of the Gunnison River known for its gold-medal waters. We camped in a delightful overhang of cliffs, where the river was crystal clear and lively and the rapids abundant.

On our first day out, I watched Tavenner land and release one rainbow trout after another. He approached fly fishing as kind of a cross between religion and reincarnation.

"You need to become the fish," he explained excitedly to me. "You visualize what the *fish* wants, not what you want. You let your intuitive side override the thinking part of your brain."

"Right-brained fishing?" I inquired.

He considered a moment. "Yes. You're triggering their fish

archetypes which have evolved over generations to strike at a certain object. So you have to be intuitive to anticipate what they want. Thinking is a slowing-down process. Action and reaction. That's why it's spiritual."

"So what's the first commandment?" I asked.

"Presentation," he replied. "Presentation is everything."

"Ah," I nodded knowingly, not having the faintest clue what he meant. But I learned.

The Gunnison happens to be perfect for trout. It is not just one river, but a series of them layered into a single, sometimes chaotic unit. At the bottom is the river of sand, then there is the river of water above, and above that a river of air. Within those three are the rivers of life: the snails, insects, snakes, frogs, cephalopods, nutria, beaver, otter, and then the eagles and ospreys that swoop down to snatch the top of the water food chain, the trout.

Trout, as everyone knows, are wily, skitterish and fine-tasting. They are the highest predator in the river, except for the fly fishermen, who attempt to imitate what the trout are eating, often at great trouble and expense, and talk about the "hatches" as if they were Saint's Days. It so happened that the Gunnison had just seen one of the biggest hatches of stone flies, and as a result the trout had "shoulders." Anyway, that's what Mama told me.

"How can a trout have shoulders?" I asked. "They don't even have necks."

"They're hogs," she replied. "Fat and sassy." Mama goes for only two kinds of fish—hogs and lunkers. These are left-over terms from her bass days, and they're self-explanatory.

Of course, fly fishing has a language of its own—a litany as oblique as any service in Latin. Tavenner was well-versed in the arcane terminology. He spoke to us of P.M.D., which at first I assumed was some kind of insect P.M.S., a femme fly in a nasty mood. It turned out to be a Pale Morning Dun. I was relieved P.M.S. had not invaded the bug world.

Later he announced that he was going out nymphing and invited us to come along. Visions of young things flitting through the wild Colorado woods, with Tavenner, his ponytail flapping, in hot pursuit raced through my mind.

"I'll be using a common nymph," he added, as if in explanation. Dang it, I thought, *there's vulgar ones.* Then he talked about the prince. I thought the prince would probably be the one after the nymphs, but no, this guy's made of green hare's ear, imitating an emerging caddis. Only a trout would go for a green hairy fake prince, I thought. No, wait a minute—I've dated a few of those myself.

"Of course, we could use the Girdle Bitch," Mama suggested helpfully.

"What!" I exclaimed, summoning from the past nightmarish visions of my large aunts with too-tight corsets under their cotton dresses spraddled over lawn chairs in the shade after too much pecan pie at our family reunions. Seeing my expression, Mama explained that a Girdle Bitch was just another fly—a Bitch Creek Nymph with Spandex legs. Even the explanations were surreal.

"A lot of people don't tie Girdle Bitches with Spandex legs, but I do," Mama said proudly. "They're ugly—but I've caught fish on them."

I took her word for it.

Naturally, I made all the first-timer faux pas on our initial foray to the river.

In fact, the list of my sins is excruciatingly extensive:

1. I called the custom-built, monographed, nine-foot, light-weight, five-hundred-dollar graphite fly rod Tavenner let me use "a pole." "Lemme see that pole," I said cheerfully. His face contorted in pain.

2. I asked Tavenner why he didn't have "a bigger bobber." "That's a strike indicator," he informed me, his voice dripping disgust.

3. I put my arms inside my chest-waders. (I was trying to pull up my socks.)

4. I fell over in the rushing water with both my arms inside my chest-waders. I needn't tell you how bad a mistake *that* was. The river ran over me. Baptized me. In the name of the Mother, the Sun, and the Holy Float. It would have drowned me, too, if Tavenner hadn't caught me as I washed downstream and dragged me to shore by my suspenders.

5. I hooked my hair, my leg, my backside. Mama and Tavenner moved several hundred paces upriver from me.

6. I fished with moss. "Clean the moss off your fly every second cast, why don't you, honey?" suggested Mama in a kindly fashion, after noticing my half-hour's moss-casting.

7. I forgot to look at the strike indicator. I was too occupied watching my mother jerking in hogs and lunkers repeatedly. Suddenly, I had a strike myself, but the fish was gone in a flash when I didn't set the hook.

8. When we rafted downstream to fish the riffles, I actually succeeded in hooking *and landing* a rainbow trout, but got so excited I fell out of the boat—onto my fish. It swished a lot under me. Scared me. Scared the fish, too, no doubt. I could be the only fisherman who has ever squashed her fish in the water.

But for all these transgressions and more, I did penance. All fly fishermen do, whether they sin or not. Standing in freezing water for long periods of time: that's the flagellation part of the religion. When I got to where I enjoyed it, I began to worry.

Mama, however, had risen to a higher plane—Cardinal status at least, if not exactly Joan of Arc. She cut an intriguing figure out on the river, constantly moving with the smooth, fluid motion of an expert caster. It was meditational. Every once in a while the rhythm would be interrupted with an abrupt yelp, which meant she'd caught another lunker with shoulders.

All this spirituality hadn't been free, of course. Like all sects, this one included tithing. Why, one rooster neck for making flies is forty dollars, and one packet of green hare's ear hair, twelve bucks. And when you add to it the state-of-the-art graphite rods, reels, vests, waders, hats, bags, nets, and so on, it makes you gasp.

Yet the most unique item Tavenner had sold to my mother, which she wore around her neck like a vestment and never removed, was the least expensive. This was the fisherman's tool lanyard, a tool originally used for bait rigging while fishing offshore, but adapted for fly fishermen. It's particularly advantageous for deep-river waders and floaters because all the tools you need are visible and securely fastened on a lanyard around your neck, handier than having to dig through a tackle box or vest.

The typical setup includes a Swiss army knife or small scissors to cut line, hemostats to remove hooks, small needle-nose pliers to debarb hooks, a leader straightener, a leader sink, silicone floatant, a hook file, and finally, a stomach pump.

This last item was a revelation. I've seen some pretty outrageous things done in the name of sport, like whacking off bull parts in Spain, but trout stomach pumping has to be at the top. With the first trout Mama caught, she, without warning, began to suck all the insides out of the thing.

"What are you *doing to that fish?*" I shouted, making her leap in alarm.

"Pumping out the little bugger's belly," she replied nonchalantly. "You have to see what they're eating, you know," she added instructively.

I *hadn't* known that. "There must be a better way," I insisted.

She examined the green stuff in the tube. "Shoot, nothing but moss," she muttered and dropped the dripping mess onto her shirt front, where the stain spread.

"Think I'll get another cup of coffee," I gagged.

You can renounce all these worldly goods and take your fly fishing back to its simplest state, as the ascetics do in any religion. For instance, Tavenner told us about a client he'd once guided on the river who fished with spines from the barrel cactus with a fly tied on. This man, Tavenner said, had explored the length and breadth of fly fishing and discovered its pure, natural form.

"That's the largest wad of horse crap I ever heard," Mama exclaimed, staring at Tavenner. She was about to say something else, but just then one of those Amazing But True Fish Things happened. I got a strike, a good one. All of us turned our attention to the end of my line. The fish dived straight down, then shot straight up, hit the water, and flew several feet into the air. It was so fast, I couldn't keep the tension on my line. The huge rainbow coiled high in the air for a moment, glistening, poised, droplets of water spraying outward and catching the sun. Then, facing its hunter, the fish turned and spat the fly out in my face. It was well-timed and altogether amazing. I heard Mama laugh.

"That fish has been in this game before," she remarked

drolly.

"That fish just made my trip," I sighed lightly with satisfaction. Gazing at the rippling water, I reflected, "It's funny, but in all my years of fishing, the ones I remember most are the big ones I've lost."

And somehow, that seemed a perfect benediction for the day.

E. ANNIE PROULX

Somewhere With Sven

T HE CRITICAL geometry in the camping trip is the other person. I am not a Type-A camper—more of a B minus—but my friend Sven, with whom I have tented for a decade, falls off the far end of the scale. Triple Z. His attitude would give a frisson of danger to a wienie roast in a state park. I swear each trip is the last, but back home, all cracked fingernails and gravel burns, I know I've been somewhere.

Sven attracts trouble the way some dogs attract porcupines; that is, he looks for it and finds it. But never does Sven get a snoutful of quills. When he was fifteen years old, he reported to an Iowa warehouse to start a summer job in the packing department. A nearsighted dispatcher said, "About time you got here," threw him a set of keys and told him to drive the semi at the loading dock to Minneapolis. Late in the day young Sven came back, load delivered, truck unscathed. The dispatcher, hysterical with relief, pressed a handful of cigars on him. Bubble gum would have been the thing.

Not long ago Sven renounced a career as a small-town newspaper editor and sat for the bar exam. This mental calisthenic took place in the meeting hall of the Loyal Order of the Vomerine Fang or some such lodge with the requisite number of long tables to accommodate the candidates. A proctor passed out the examination questions, and the scribbling began. But Sven's attention was drawn to a stuffed pike on the wall. He looked at it, couldn't get started. At last he got up and approached the pike. His fingers grazed its flank. The pike fell onto the examination table in a billow of dust, plaster, flaked paint, desiccated scales and threadlike motes that one of the candidates (a specialist in environmental hazards) identified as asbestos. While the agitated candidates and proctors mopped at the table, Sven started writing. He finished three-quarters of an hour before anyone else and with the second-highest score. It is this artless recovery in the atmosphere of chaos that makes Sven a nonpareil camping companion.

Years ago, when both Sven and I were getting serious about fly fishing, we met a fellow who tied uncommon flies. We ordered handfuls. Mine went astray in the mail, but Sven got his fifty assorted. He laid them out on a black cloth and gloated over them. The season opened, and Sven tossed his drugstore fly rod into his car, put the folded cloth on the seat beside him and headed for a river. Out on the interstate he suddenly had to take another look at the flies, pulled into a rest area, got out and spread the black cloth on the hood. Beautiful. He was tempted to lick one.

Back on the road, bowling along at eighty-five, he glanced at the passenger seat. The black cloth was not there. Nor was it on the hood. By cutting across the median into the southbound lane and working the exits, he managed to skid into the rest area just as a tour bus pulled out. There were his flies, all of them, embedded in the rear tires of the bus, ready to lure whatever road trout were out there. But the loss was really a gain, he said, for he bought a vise and someday will begin to tie his own flies.

One spring Sven and I planned to fish a certain Maine lake. Sven insisted we go in his tiny "fishing car." (He associated my old truck with the painful memories of a Newfoundland trip that had involved bears, dry waffles, storms, inaccessible salmon water and a meeting with a compulsive furnace salesman in a rubber dinghy.)

He readied his fishing car by raking out piles of old newspaper—rediscovering his baseball jacket, his cap surmounted with the beer-can holder and long, flexible straw, forty or fifty loose dog biscuits and some Styrofoam coffee containers (none empty, as Sven likes cold coffee). He drained the oil—funny color—and dumped in four quarts of new.

We lashed my canoe onto his fishing car. The ensemble looked like a sub roll balanced on a meatball and handled the same way. Six hours of driving and we were at the jump-off town; beyond, another six hours of ruinous, rock-strewn road. Sven said, "There's something funny about second gear."

"We just passed the last garage for two hundred miles."

"I don't trust anybody but Will Bill to work on my fishing car." He stopped and looked under the hood himself.

"The spark plugs are *filthy*. Good thing I brought more." He changed them. "Look how oily these old plugs are."

The connection between spark plugs and second gear seemed remote to me, but it was his car.

In a while Sven said, "Second gear again," pointing with his unshaven chin at the hoarse sound coming from the front of the vehicle. "But we've still got the other gears."

At the lake we rammed the ailing vehicle under a shrub and set up camp. Sven fidgeted, muttered, wished Will Bill were there. He dropped the pot holder in the lake and watched it float away. It was his turn to gather firewood, but instead of an ax he had brought a handmade folk machete from Costa Rica. He demonstrated its sharpness by shaving hairs from his arm. I could see half a dozen stubbly patches between wrist and elbow; he must have been testing it all night. He flailed at a dead stick. The machete glanced off and whistled past his shin. A second blow opened one end of his tackle box. Bloody hell.

Too early in the year for a hatch, but I had my fly rod, hoping for trout. Sven flexed his ocean-weight spinning rod and swore the togue would be mesmerized by the metal hose clamp he favored as a lure. The togue were in the lake, not the river. The squaretails were in the river, not the lake, and they were not taking flies. We compromised (it was my canoe) and paddled into the river to fish the pools at the bends.

The sun beat like a mallet, the heated air quivered. An insect drifted past me and landed on the water. There was a watery commotion and a wet smacking sound. A clot of insects wavered past, and I grabbed one—a large winged ant. I rummaged through my fly case with dancing hands. A sixteen-inch brook trout seized the fly before it touched the water. There were ants in the canoe, in our hair, crawling over the paddles and gunwales, and all around us fish were lunging and gobbling. Sven tore the hose clamp off his line and tied on the bedraggled muddler rusting in his hatband, the only fly he had left after the bus incident. He cast.

"You're casting in my water," I said coldly.

He cast again, actually crossing my line.

"Get away," I shrieked. But he kept on splashing with his rotten muddler. A scene developed, both of us hurling flies at the same spot, hissing insults, deliberately lurching the canoe so the other would fall out and drown, and when one hooked a trout the other frightened it off with threatening and premature swoops of the landing net. I threw the hose clamp overboard. The whole affair was disgusting.

That evening conversation twisted into icy sneers of "Excuse *me*" and "I *hope* this doesn't *bother* you," and when the machete flashed I anticipated, with sordid pleasure, a leg amputation. When I went to rinse my wine glass and fell into the shallows, Sven laughed, and when he collided with a tarp line so forcibly it left a rope burn under his chin that made him look like the major participant in a necktie party, I laughed. It was like that for three days.

We drove out in sullen humor. Second gear snarled nonstop, and first and third were gravelly. For every five miles of travel, there was an obligatory ten-minute rest before we could go on. At one point Sven got out and stood at the side of the road with an imploring expression on his face. Logging trucks roared by like hell-bound trains.

"The people up here are cold," he said, getting back behind the wheel. What had he expected—to be hoisted atop a load of logs and portaged out?

We finally reached the jump-off town. I could see the garage sign shimmering: repairs. But as we came abreast, Sven kept going.

"The garage!" I bleated.

"I think I can make it back," he said simply.

"Make it back? It's three hundred miles."

"I got a good look at the mechanic at that garage. I didn't trust him. He looked like Robert De Niro in a greasy jumpsuit."

The car quit a few miles down the road. We pushed it to the crest of a hill and steered into a potluck town with a phone booth. Our mutual friend, Redemptio, had the hard luck to be at home after ten days of building ski lifts in the mountains.

"Sven! How's it going? . . . What? . . . *Where?* . . . My tow trailer? . . . Look, I just got back from fucking Maine! . . . I'm hungry! . . . It'll take at least six hours to get there! . . . You'll buy me *dinner?* . . . What do you mean the people up there are cold? It's *Maine,* for God's sake, of course they're cold . . . Ah, Mother of God, all right, *all right.*"

During the hours waiting for Redemptio, Sven told me, "This is how you learn who your real friends are," as though he had invented an extremely important test. The ride home in Redemptio's gritty truck, our feet resting awkwardly on chains and cables, was subdued. Redemptio didn't feel like conversation; lightning played around the edges of his eyes.

The gear problem had been laughably simple, said Sven on the telephone a few days later after a consultation with Will Bill. In preparing the fishing car for the trip he had mistakenly drained out the transmission fluid, then added four quarts of fresh engine oil to the four already there. No wonder the spark plugs dripped. No wonder the gearbox seized up.

"You mean if we'd just put in some—"

"Yes. But then we wouldn't have had dinner with Redemptio."

"Redemptio got diarrhea from the shrimp."

"Should have had the meat loaf. Listen, I've been thinking," said Sven. "Do you remember that pond two years ago where we only caught a seven-inch whitefish and in the heat wave we had to wear heavy jackets and ski stockings and gloves and head nets because the blackflies were so bad, and then later the thunderstorm in the night when the moose almost stepped on your head and you got up and slept in the back of your truck until the tree went down, and we forgot to bring any coffee?"

"You bet," I said.

"I've been thinking. We should go back there next spring."

"Not in this life."

"Well. Maybe not there, but near there. There's a place on the map that looks good. Very remote and difficult to get to."

These were the enchanting words: *remote* and *difficult*.

"My friend, yes, if we go in separate vehicles and bring separate canoes and separate tents and separate pot holders. I'll bring my own ax. You might bring Will Bill or a copy of *Car Repairs Made Easy.*"

"Will Bill'd rather fry in the electric chair than go camping. Anyway, I'm buying a heavy-duty four-wheel-drive this winter."

So the next spring I met Sven in another jump-off town near the New Brunswick border. Everything was separate. If there was another *crise de nerfs* coming, I'd have it alone in my own canoe.

He was late. Then I saw the familiar flash of turquoise, and beneath his canoe the ratty fishing car. Where was the four-wheel-drive?

"It's too new. Will Bill fixed the fishing car. It went eight hundred miles on no transmission fluid—great car."

Great car or not, it had a clearance of about eight inches, and the spring logging roads were bad.

Trouble right away. My old truck bucketed gamely through the washouts, but the fishing car got smaller and smaller in the side mirror and finally disappeared. I pulled over and waited until it came in sight, rearing like Steamboat, the 1901 bucking horse champ.

"Don't drive so fast," shouted Sven. His forehead was swollen from smashing against the windshield.

"I'm going fifteen miles an hour. If I slow down, I'll stop."

The roads narrowed and steepened, and we slid over ice, plunged into mud. The fishing car got mired too many times to count. At dark we were still fifty miles from the remote and difficult lake. We hadn't seen another vehicle for hours. The sky was dirt black, and the wind was rising.

"We ought to stop for the night." Sven's jaws cracked with yawns.

"The map shows a campsite—Big Crossover. Five or six miles. What do you say?"

Sven said something frightful. "Do you think the lake's still frozen?"

It began to rain.

When I stuck my head out of the back of the truck in the morning, it was into a sluicing downpour that would make every pothole a potential axle-buster of unknown depth. Rainwater diluted the coffee in our cups. Sven rolled up his wet tent and threw it into the fishing car.

There were interminable stretches of mean road. In the rain

it was hard to see deep washouts until we were almost in them. We carried planks to lay over sections of collapsed bridge, but the fishing car couldn't handle even the good ones without help, so it was get out, set the planks, guide the fishing car across, pick up the planks, and go on. Three or four times the fishing car spun its little wheels and had to be pulled free.

"This will just take a minute," Sven said gently every time.

Less than five miles from the lake—I could hear whistled bits of a popular Lithuanian polka coming from the fishing car—we came into a sumpy, flat section that disappeared in a blind elbow turn. We faced half a mile of ruts filled with yellow water. There was a brimful ditch on each side of the road, rippling across here and there. I put on my boots and stepped into a rut to gauge its depth, the firmness of the gravel beneath. No problem for the truck, but two inches beyond the fishing car's tolerance. Maybe we could transfer Sven's stuff. There was a terrific honking, and here came Sven without waiting for the road report. I jumped into the ditch, and the cursed fishing car, fizzing like a shooting star, drove its breast deep into the gravel between the ruts.

I have never seen a car so hung up. Only the tops of the tires showed. Sven had to crawl out the window because the lower edges of the doors were deep in the ground. All the way, from the front bumper (somewhere down there) to the exhaust pipe, the fishing car was interred.

To keep from howling, I emptied my boots, put them back on and waded toward the bend in the road to see what thrills lay beyond. The water got deeper, but the gravel at the bottom of the ruts held firm. I rounded the corner and caught my breath. The road disappeared under a pond about a hundred yards across with a merry little stream running through it. In the distance the road rose out of the watery depths. I probed with a stick. Waist-deep. I could hear falling water. To the left was a wing dam of fresh-cut brush, and below it a sturdy beaver dam.

I waded back to Sven, who was lying in the water digging hard-packed gravel from under the fishing car with a canoe paddle.

"You got any dynamite?"

"No. Redemptio's got some."

"He's in Peru, lucky for him. Quit digging, and come see what I found. The road goes under a pond. In the rain last night the beaver damned the ditch overflow."

"We'll drain the pond, then dig out the car," said Sven.

For three hours we worked at it. We tore out the wing dam and breached the beaver dam. There was a spectacular gout of water. On our knees, then lying on our sides with one ear in the water, we dug and clawed yards of gravel from under the fishing car. We drained the ruts by gouging out small ditches to the big ditch with our boot heels and held back new inflow with temporary dams made from the planks. Then we jerked the fishing car half a mile back to a pull-off. It was wordlessly understood to be the end of the line for the damn thing. The rain faded.

"Now, let's load my gear and canoe into your truck, and we'll drive through that pond." Sven rubbed his hands.

"If we stall, we've had the radish." I'd never driven down an invisible road through deep water.

"Yeah," said Sven. "Let's go."

There was the sound of a distant engine drawing near. A game warden slewed up in his green pickup and looked at us, wringing with rain and sweat, slobbered in mud, our raw hands bleeding. We said we were trying to get to the lake. He stared at the mud-coated fishing car, studied the drained ruts, the lowered pond, then drove through, rooster tails of water shooting up, and disappeared in the far spruce.

"He was cute."

"I thought he looked like Larry Bird with a Vermont face-lift."

I steered the truck into the pond, traced the curve of the road by the mud bloom stirred in the warden's passage, and held my breath. As the truck chugged up the far side onto the dry road again, I whooped and banged on the truck door, and Sven grinned.

"You know—"

"Yeah."

"Digging gravel with the paddles was the worst."

"You got it."

The weather turned to sweet milk; we watched the wind drive the ice down the lake in a thousand-acre blanket of clinking, rattling, tinkling crystals, a sound like someone sweeping broken glass on the grand scale; I met and lost the trout of my dreams; and there were flaming meteors in the night.

On the way back we discovered the beavers had rebuilt the dam. The pond was twice as wide and neck-deep.

"What *is* a Vermont facelift?"

"Three clothespins at the back of the head."

Like I say, you've got to get the right person for the memorable camping trips.

LORIAN HEMINGWAY

Walk on Water for Me

I TAKE FISH personally, the
way I have my life, like a sacrament. This is my body. Eat of it.
This is my blood. Drink. I imagine this reverence is what they
want of me. The alchemists made an eyewash (collyrium) of fish,
believing it would bring omniscience. I've tried to envision the
process: cooking the fish, as the alchemists instructed, until it
"yellowed," mashing it into a crumbly pulp, mixing it with water and then filling the eyes with this paste so one might gaze
with as much dimension as trout in a clear stream. But as with all
things in alchemy it was the process that mattered, the final result never as important as the ritual preceding it.

Knowing fish is a process. I have been acquainting myself for forty years. To know fish you have to have been intimate, the way the alchemists were. The first fish I ever caught was a baby bass netted from a deep Mississippi ravine I lived near during summer. It was my refuge, that ravine, a place of discovery, revealer of miracles, its depth filled with a heavy current of reddish-brown water during the spring floods, its clay bottom dried to a pockmarking of deep holes by mid-July. I was tirelessly curious when I was young, bound inextricably to all natural mysteries beyond four walls, nervous and jumpy if made to sit too long indoors, recalcitrant once sprung. I'd watched this particular fish for days, trapped in a pothole in the ravine, swimming in a quick panic from one side to the other, instinctively seeking a tributary leading from its footwide prison. I empathized, imagined myself locked in my room for days, dizzy and breathless from ensuing claustrophobia, frantic enough to pull up the flooring with my bare hands. I understood feeling trapped, my life then nothing more than a crash course in how to escape.

After a few days the water in the pothole had diminished by half and grew so thick with ravine mud that the fish hung motionless in the ooze, its gills laboring for the oxygen it needed. On my knees I stared into the hole, goldfish net in hand, thinking it was evil what I was about to do, snatch a living creature from its habitat and bring it, luckless, into my own. I remember the delicate, thin striping on it flanks as I lifted it, unprotesting, from the muck, and how soft and filmy the skin felt as I stroked a finger along his length. I remember, too, how my heart raced as I dropped the fish into a jar, watched him sink quickly and then just as quickly take his first breath in a new world. Within moments he was moving through the jar as manically as he had the pothole days before. I had given resurrection in a pint of water, become God to a fish. Years later I would remember that moment as one of grace.

Fish became my fascination, and began to appear in dreams, their shadows deep in dark water, cruising, fins breaking the surface from time to time, a teasing swirl of movement as I stood on shore with net or rod or hands poised to strike. In one dream I stood before a pool of monster fish with bare hands greedy, my fingertips singing the way a line does when it's pulled free from the spool. As I leaned forward, a shape would slide deliberately beneath my reach, and I would lunge into water that was dense and thick as oil, only to come up soaked and empty-handed.

I don't know now that the dreams had to do with catching fish, but rather with some unconscious, archetypal need. I have consulted Jung on this one for the obvious, loaded symbolism. I have even dreamt, in these later years, of Jung, standing atop the stone fortress of his tower at Bollingen, fly rod in hand, a wooden piscatorial carving dangling from his leader line. He smiles in the dream, proud of himself. He did say water is the unconscious and that fish are a Christ symbol. I deduce then, from these two boldly fitting pieces, that I am at times fishing for Jesus, or in some way, in recent dreams, dry-flying for Christ. I like the simplicity of it, the directness. I like that it speaks to Christian and Hedon alike.

But during those Mississippi summers I paid little attention to dreams, mesmerized then by a world filled with fish, snakes, turtles, toads and lizards, anything remotely amphibian. I progressed from netting bass to catfishing with a bobber and worm, frittering away entire days on the banks of muddy lakes, certain, always, that the fish lived dead center in the middle of the lake, assuming the notion that the truly elusive spend their time where we can never hope to reach them. To cast where they hid became my ambition, and once mastered I understood that fish went wherever they damned well pleased, unimpressed by my clumsy form hurling hooks into their midst, immune to my need to know them.

I had patience, the sort I suspect God has with people like me. It was nothing to be skunked for days on end. I lived in perpetual hope of seeing that wayward shimmy of the bobber, then the quick dip and tug that signaled I had made contact with aliens. At that time in my life this was my social interaction. I talked to the fish hidden deep in the ponds and streams I visited, trying to imagine what they saw beneath those mirrored surfaces and reasoned it was hunger and not stupidity that made them take bait so crudely hitched to an obvious weapon. Compassion surfaced. I pictured scores of starving fish grubbing for worms only to be duped into death by my slipshod cunning. When I'd reel them to shore I'd cry at what I'd done, at the sight of the hook swallowed to the hilt, at the flat, accusing eyes of the fish, and then I'd club them with a Coke bottle, the heavy green kind with the bottling company's name on the bottom. No one ever said there was another way to do it. In Mississippi, there was the hook, the worm and the bobber, a holy trinity on a hot day in August—low-maintenance fishing I call it now. My guilt was usually pushed aside by their quick death beneath the bottle, and eating what I had caught seemed to remove the shame considerably.

My favorite fishing hole—I look back on it now as Mississippi's version of Mecca—was a place that to this day I am certain only one other knew of, the landowner who'd barbwired it off and posted a huge, hand-painted sign along the fence— Warning: SNAKES. Roaming deep in a pine woods in rural Hinds County one summer afternoon, I came upon the pond, the edges of it rising in volcanic fashion from the otherwise flat land.

I was accustomed only to ponds that were slipped like sinkholes into the surrounding pastureland, and as I made my way up the slight incline of earth, hands grasping the barbwire delicately, I beheld, not a rock quarry as I had expected, but instead a perfectly black pool of water, its dimensions no greater than those of an average swimming pool. At first I could not believe the color of the fish who were pushing to the surface, dozens of them, nosing one into another, their bodies as opalescent as pearls, and huge, their lengths dissolving into the shadow of the pond. I had never seen albino catfish, had never seen *any* white fish, and thought for a brief, illogical moment that they had been segregated from their darker mates simply because of their color. In Mississippi, then, it fit.

To have called this pond a fishing hole is misleading. I never actually fished its waters, too mesmerized by the cloudlike shapes that moved without sound through the deep pond, believing, beyond all fishing reason, that to catch them would bring the worst sort of luck. So I watched, alone in the woods with these mutants, some days prodding their lazy bodies with a hickory stick, which they rubbed against curiously, and on others merely counting the number of laps they made around the pond in an afternoon, hypnotized by the rhythm they made tracing one circle upon another.

The fish were as truly alien as my starkest imaginings, and I became convinced they were telepathic, reading my thoughts with such ease I had no need to speak to them. I called these sojourns "visiting the fish gods," my treks to that mysterious water that had no business existing in dry woods, and took into adulthood the memory of them, as if they were a talisman, granting me privileges and luck in the fishing world others could only dream of.

As I grew older I began to think of fish as mine. I'd been in close touch with them long enough to develop something that I believed went beyond rapport and came, in time, to border on feudalism. Fishing became far more than sport or communion. It began to develop the distinct earmarkings of a life's goal. No longer content to watch and prod, no longer in command of patience, I lived to fish, becoming, in my own mind, a fishing czarina, my luck with rod, reel and bait phenomenal.

Self-taught in the simple mechanisms of spinning gear, I had perfected a bizarre way of holding the reel and rod upside down while casting and retrieving. It is something I have never been able to undo, the habit of flipping the rod over before I cast worn into my nerve pathways like my image of Christ as a skinny Caucasian. Years late someone told me I cast like a child. So what. It never marred my accuracy, and in fact I was a little pleased childhood habits had stalked me this far. I was also told "any idiot can catch fish with a dead piece of flesh and a bent nail." I *was* an idiot, but smug in my idiocy, refusing to let go of sure-fire methods I'd known as a kid in Mississippi. Holding true to my fundamentalist, country fishing ways, I began to gain a reputation for being the only person certain, on an outing, to catch fish. An attitude surfaced as rapidly as fish to my bait. Men were forced to regard me now, but warily, as I moved within their circles, trying always to outdo them. Gone was the solitary fishing of my childhood, the secret visits with fish gods. I had become competitive.

I cannot place the exact time when my fishing innocence turned streetwalker tough, when imagined power over the waters of childhood turned to a calculating game, but I suspect it was when I discovered that good-old-boy fishing and beer went hand-in-hand. I'd been drinking plenty before I became truly obsessed with bait and tackle, but now I began articles I wrote on the subject with lines like "Nothing like a cold six-pack in the morning," causing my editors to wince and accuse me of writing manuscripts "afloat in beer."

I took to drinking the way I had to that ravine in summer, daily, and the false tough-girl attitude it fostered launched me into an arena that included the truly elusive, monsters who swim leagues deep in saltwater. Armed with the fishing world's equivalent of an elephant gun, I hunted tropical waters for marlin, shark, tuna, tarpon and barracuda, catching them all, tearing muscles and breaking blood vessels while in battle, but anesthetized to the pain because my six-pack in the morning had now become a full case in a five-hour stint.

The popular image of a fisherman sitting on the bank on a quiet Sunday afternoon, pole propped against a rock, cold beer in hand, contemplating, was about as close to what I did on the water as Andy Warhol is to Degas. On board I was a one-armed windmill in one hundred-knot winds, my hand dipping in the cooler for a drink as fast as I hauled fish on deck. I was Macho Woman. Back off. This is the life, I told myself a lot during those days, the idea that one occasionally encounters periods of grace eluding me entirely.

Still, I was ashamed when my prey would slide alongside the boat, exhausted, beaten to near death. I'd release them, guiltily, my hand still reaching involuntarily for the Coke bottle, now a flimsy aluminum can, worthless as it turned out, for any feat of strength. People would slap me on the back and say things like, "You fish like a man. You drink like a man," offerings that in the light of what I was to become, seem almost comical now. But at the time I considered it an honor, posing willingly with other people's four hundred-pound slabs of dead marlin, beer can held aloft, grinning crookedly, a mutant now compared to that girl bent over the potholes, goldfish net in hand.

For several years I was flat-out on the gonzo stage of fishing, where any method of felling fish was acceptable. I never batted an eye at ten-pound teasers rigged to the transoms of forty-foot sportsfishermen. The anchor-sized saltwater reels looked normal to me, and fifty-pound test, what the hell. I had lost sight of that first delicate intimacy, the tiny bass swimming clearly in my see-through jar of river water. I no longer practiced communion, but sacrilege. My life, as well as my fishing, had turned brutal.

I prefer the confessional to the cross, figuring if I own to enough treachery I will be spared in a moment of mercy, like that bass in the ravine. When I quit drinking—finally—after an eight-year period of uncommon buoyancy on sea as well as land, my liver shot, my eyes as yellowed as the fish the alchemists sought for insight—I quit the gonzo lifestyle. "Blind drunk" is not a phrase without meaning, and to me it came to mean that I had been blind, almost irrevocably, not only to the damage lev-eled in my own life, but to the life beneath those waters that came so frequently in dreams.

Dead cold sober now, I took up fly fishing. Not on the same day, certainly, because the shakes wrack you for a while and all you're really good for is mixing paint. I'd held a fly rod only once during my fish killing days, off the coast of Islamorada during tarpon season, while fishing with legendary guide Jimmie All-bright. In the saltwater fishing world, *guides* and *anglers* are leg-endary, never the fish who serve them. After meeting enough of the old masters, I came to the conclusion that to become legend-ary all one needed was to catch oversized fish and not die from sunstroke or lip cancer, tie a few exotic-looking flies, cast phe-nomenal distances against the wind and remain steadfastly la-conic when a novice is on board. What I remember most of the first fly fishing experience is a lot of yeps and nopes directed at my questions, the fly line cinched tightly around my ankles after a bad cast, and a sunburn that bubbled the skin on the tops of my ears. It was a waste of energy, I figured. I didn't get the point. All that whipping and hauling and peering into the distance just reminded me of bad Westerns.

But something happens when you get purified, take the cure, lob your body onto another plane of perception. Without a beer in hand fly fishing seemed far more appealing to me than it had when I'd been trolling with bait big enough to eat. Back then I'd called it effete, elitist, prissy, egg-sucking. I figured the entire state of Montana was crawling with seven million people who looked exactly like Robert Redford, all of them hefting custom fly rods. Now in a completely altered state of mind, I began to notice the grace involved in a simple cast, how the arm of a good angler was merely an extension of the fly rod. I studied the art a little, secretly, not yet ready to be labeled a wimp.

About the time I was reading Izaak Walton's *The Compleat Angler*, I got a call from Florida writer and fly fishing guide Randy Wayne White asking me to fly fish on his PBS-syndicated fishing show, "On The Water." I didn't tell the man I couldn't cast spare change into the hand of a willing Hare Krishna, much less fly cast for tarpon, which was what he had in mind.

"Sure," I told him, eager, as always, for a new opportunity to humiliate myself. "I've caught tarpon before," neglecting to mention it was with an orange Day-Glo bobber and a live mullet. I wanted to be prepared and figured with all I'd read on the subject I could learn the basics in half an hour of hands-on practice. So after taking a quick lesson in a downtown Seattle park, I flew south.

I was soon sitting anchored off a mangrove island on Florida's west coast with Randy. Randy Wayne White is what you would call a burly man, built like a fireplug with forearms the girth of oak saplings, an image that belies his physical grace, and particularly his ability with a fly rod.

"Where'd you learn to cast, Lorian?" he was asking politely as he grinned into the sun and the PBS camera, while I whizzed a live pilchard past his head. He hadn't seen me fly cast yet because I'd begged off after watching Randy sail his line eighty feet toward a school of feeding redfish. Nah, I'd told myself after watching a redfish pounce the fly, this won't do. I was out of my element entirely, beerless, baitless, naked.

"I never did learn," I told him, my back to the camera as I slung another pilchard into the mangroves. "Amazing, isn't it," I said, "what you can teach yourself." Randy nodded, his eyes losing hope. This exchange never survived the edited version of the show's tape, and in subsequent shots the camera gently panned away into the mangroves, or to the pelicans flying above, as I cast upside down and reeled backwards, dragging whole mangrove tubers boatside.

The second day out we headed in Randy's flats boat for the coast of Boca Grande where scores of tarpon were rolling on the surface of the water. Randy slapped a custom, saltwater fly rod into my hand and said, "Go for it, Lorian!"

Go for what? I remember thinking. For what, for Christ's sake. It was enough in a ten-foot chop on a three-foot wide boat to merely right myself and stand there lurching starboard, portside, fore and aft, like one of those sand-weighted plastic clowns that lean wa-ay over but never quite go down. I viewed the wallowing tarpon at eye level and imagined offering my lunch as chum into the churning water.

"There're hundreds of them, Lorian. Hundreds. Go ahead and cast, " Randy called from the stern.

I think I pulled maybe six inches of line from the reel before I noticed the particular leaden quality of the sky just north, south, east and west of us, as Randy yelled. "Two o'clock. Tarpon at two o'clock."

The sky at two o'clock looked like midnight with the occasional atomically bright lightening bolt shearing the blackness.

I'm no fan of lightning while in an open boat, no fan of lightning while wearing a rubber suit in a six-foot-deep cellar. It's a phobia of mine—call it silly—one that's rampant, unchecked, paralyzing.

"Graphite," my head said. "You're holding a goddamned graphite rod." PUT IT DOWN. What they don't tell you about fly rods is that they're superb electrical conductors, right up there with copper. I chucked the rod in Randy's direction, hit the deck and yelled "Drive!" about the time a bolt struck dead center off the bow and the air turned crispy crackly with electricity. I could feel the hair on my neck and arms rise up.

I spent the beat-your-kidneys-to-Jello ride back to shore face down in the boat, my nails tearing at Randy's left calf, hissing Hail Marys, as lightning popped in the water around us.

"Next time I see you, I'll give you a casting lesson," Randy told me the next day, as I wandered around randomly kissing the ground, his hand, the cheeks of strangers, stunned to be alive.

"Like fun," I said.

It took a while before I could look at a fly rod again without itching to buy life insurance. But the dreams returned, this time of pink speckled trout in blue streams, less threatening than tarpon in boiling, black water, and I thought, sure, that's where I belong, in a trout stream wearing waders and a nifty fly vest displaying hand-tied flies, maybe a telescoping depth wand strapped at my hip, Swiss army knife dangling from that ring on the vest pocket. That's me all right, the Orvis girl. And since I figured you don't have to be a ballerina to dance, I took up casting again, practicing in my back yard—and a one and a two—secretive and clumsy, the cat my only witness. Somewhere around my fortieth birthday my husband Jeff had given me a new rod and reel, complete with weight-forward line, and I took to the business of learning to cast as earnestly as I take to anything, which means if I don't master it on the second or third try, I quit, stick out my lower lip and glare.

I had achieved mid-beginner status (capable of placing the fly on the water by wadding the line in my fist and heaving it) when Jeff and I took a trip to the Salmon River in Idaho. I had taken fish there years before, six-pack in hand, spinning gear in the other, dragging the rocks—twenty-four trout in half a day, my finest hour, but drunk when I did it so maybe the count's off by half. I wanted to return to make amends, to take a trout clean and easy without the heavy artillery.

The Salmon is a beautiful stretch of water, clear, relatively shallow and fast, unlike the slow, clay-weighted waters of Mississippi. When I first moved to the Northwest I was amazed you could see so deeply into the water and would sit for hours on a river shore staring at the rocks beneath. Jeff, on the other hand, grew up with this purity, which may explain why it seems to be in his blood to fish these waters, and fish them well, in fact better than anyone has a right to. He has the sort of luck with a fly rod that I used to have with bait, a fact that has compelled me to accuse him of actually robbing me of fish-luck, a high crime in our marriage.

Our first day on the river I'd waded in bare-legged and was fishing generally the same area of water as Jeff, but politely upstream so the fish would get to me first, when his luck (he calls it skill) kicked in. He'd released six fish before I'd even gotten my

fly damp. Normally I handled such flagrant displays with sto-
icism, wanting to keep my image as a good sport intact, but this
day was different. I'd returned to waters that had blessed me
once with uncanny luck, to waters that had kindly not swallowed
me whole as I'd staggered through them, and all I wanted was
that brief, immortal contact with aliens, the way I'd known it
when I was a kid, new and simple. I was obsessed that day with
taking a fish on fly. I'd read A.J. and Norman. I'd gone to the
outdoor shows. Nothing seemed more perfect or vital than the
feel of a trout on the end of that nerve-sensitive line. I'd felt how
mere water current could electrify the line, transforming it to a
buzzing high-voltage wire, and I wanted some of that magic.

"Yee—ha!" Jeff yelled from down river as he released another perfect form into the water.

I false cast and hooked my chin.

I could feel them all around me, the sense of them, fish moving the current in swirls around my bare ankles, fish swimming
between my thighs. I inched my way in Jeff's direction, watching
his fly line thread out before him and then drop like a whisper
onto the water.

I got within twenty feet of the man and flung my line in an
awkward sidecast right where I'd seen his last fish surface. I
waited. I prayed. I watched. I peered. Nothing.

My husband is someone who takes athletic grace for granted,
figuring it's something we all can achieve in time.

"Your presentation's wrong," he told me.

Had I read about this? I searched my memory.

"My what," I said, coming up blank.

"The way you're putting the fly down. It's wrong."

Well, what the hell. It was enough, I thought, to get the fly
in the water. Who could resist after that. And when did fish get

so picky, worrying about presentation, the particular color of a hackle. With worms there had been no guesswork. Eat this tasty sucker, you cretin, I was thinking as I fingered a rubber worm I'd stashed in my vest pocket.

"Fish are color-blind," I said with some authority, apropos of nothing.

"So," he said in that way he has that tells me he's already written a book about it.

To illustrate presentation, Jeff whipped off another perfect cast. A trout rose to his fly, and bingo, the water around us was alive. I hated him.

"Maybe it's my fly," I said.

I waded over to him and switched rods, thinking, Okay you, give me that magic wand, we'll see who catches fish.

"Yours casts so easily," he said as he set the line in motion.

Wham. I swear to God that fish hit the fly in mid-air.

"Nothing's wrong with your fly," he told me as he released the biggest trout of the day.

"That's it," I said, stomping toward shore as gracefully as possible in four feet of water. I'd snatched my rod from him and threw it on the bank when I emerged, soaked and cold, as pissed as I'd ever been.

"I thought you were a good sport," I heard him calling from the river.

There, I'd blown it. Years of cultivating an image, gone.

"Go to hell," I yelled. "Go straight to hell, you and your stupid fly rod, you jinx. Jinx! Ever since I've fished with you I've caught nothing. Not a goddamned thing. You took all my luck, and now you rub my nose in it. I'll never fish with you again. I swear to God."

I sat down on the bank and literally stomped my feet, hands

clenched into fists at my sides, my heartbeat clearly audible in my temples. I'd heard about people like me. Poor sports. Whiners. Lunatics.

"It's just your technique." The wind carried his words so that "technique" seemed to be underlined, and I shouted back, "Eat your technique. Eat it, you hear!"—a response I thought fair at the time.

It was then I saw the naked man in the raft drifting past, fly rod poised in mid-air. Ordinarily, naked would have been enough, but as I watched more closely I noticed he was throwing his rod tip up to twelve o'clock and then waiting for a beat before following through with the forward cast. During that beat the line straightened out behind him, unfurling slowly from the arc it made as he brought the rod forward. Again he cast, my own personal naked instructor, oblivious to me on the bank, and again with the same hesitation. Some technique, I thought, peering in Jeff's direction to see if he'd noticed the man. Nah. Naked women could have been skydiving into a bull's eye on his head and he'd have kept on casting. I watched the man cast another perfect length of line and discovered my arm moving involuntarily, following his motions. I watched his wrist. Hardly a bend in it as he pointed the rod arrow-straight in the direction of the unfurling line. At that moment something settled into place, the way it did that one time I bowled a strike, and I saw the whole process, not as frantic thrashing and whipping, but as one liquid motion, seamless and intact. It was the way, I thought, I should have always fished, naked, tethered to the water by a floating umbilicus, aware.

I spent the rest of the day practicing on a dirt back road, heaving that line at first as if it were a shotput. When it would drop in a dead puddle at the end of my rod I'd try again, remembering the vision of that man in the raft, his perfect rhythm, the way he seemed to notice nothing but his line as it spun out above the water. I kept trying against what I considered rather hefty odds until I had my line singing in the air and pulling out the slack around my feet as if it were ribbon shot from a rifle. I grew calm from the effort, a way I'd not remembered being for years. I looked at my hands, steady as rocks, as they rose above my head, left hand experimenting with a double haul. Hey, I thought, I might get good at this.

That evening at dusk I caught my first fish on a fly, a beauty I watched rise in a quick thrash, greedily, as if he'd been waiting all day for my one ratty fly, frayed and battered from the day's practice, but oddly noble. It's all I wanted, that one fish, electric on the end of my line, and, God, how I could feel him, his jumpy on-and-off current carrying all the way up my arm. How do you do, I felt like saying, it's been a long time. I wet my hand and cradled his girth in my palm. Such a nice feeling. Moist, alive, not slimy the way we're taught to think. I pulled some water through his gills and released the fly from his lip, delicately, no sweat, and watched as he fluttered and then dove in a quick zig zag, deep into the stream. For an instant I remembered the delicate feel of the baby bass as I slopped him into the jar of river water, then the fish gods, white and huge, circling the perimeter of the pond, aware, perhaps, of nothing more than the rhythm their movement created, and in that instant, I too, here in the clear water of an Idaho stream, understood rhythm, but as if it were the steady beat of childhood fascination returned.

In my new dream there is the same dark pool from childhood but its expanse reaches from the very tip of my feet to the horizon in all directions, its surface flat as undisturbed bathwater, the shapes beneath it perfectly formed now, truly fishlike and sharply defined, the tails like so many Geisha fans slapping left and then right in unison, a metronomic rhythm setting forth visible currents beneath the water that never break the calm glassiness above. I marvel at the dance, watch the fish line up, nose to tail, in a perfect circle, swimming faster and faster. I look to my empty hands and realize my husband stands to my left ready to make a cast with my new white lightning rod. I say, "Give it to me. Now," and cast a Royal Coachman out to Jesus. "Come on boy," I call across the pool, "walk on water for me." The fly taps the skin of the water, and the circle of fish shatters like beads in a kaleidoscope, bathing me in light.

GRETCHEN LEGLER

Fishergirl

IAM SPEEDING across Nebraska on a train, on my way to Salt Lake City from St. Paul to meet my mother. We are going to travel the "Anasazi Circle," driving through Utah, Colorado, New Mexico and Arizona to see the ruins of ancient pueblos—Hovenweep, Chaco Canyon, Canyon de Chelly and Mesa Verde. Early in our planning my mother told me that my father would not be able to accompany us because he would not have time off. "You know," I said to her, "this is just for us. Me and you." She said she knew that from the start, but that she didn't want to put it that way to him. "Maybe you'll go on a trip like this with him someday," she said.

It saddens me that I can hardly imagine my father and me in a car together, traveling the West, staying in hotels, eating at roadside cafes, sharing small details of our lives. The only thing we have ever done together is fish. Fishing is the way we have known each other, and slenderly, silently, even then. When we fish, I am Fishergirl, still eighteen and living at home, and he is my fishing father. Beyond these stories we have written for ourselves, beyond these stories we have written for and on each other, the rest of who we are seems to fall tragically away.

There is a picture of me, taken by my brother Austin, in which I am dressed up as a fly fisher. I am eighteen years old, and I am on my first fly-fishing trip to Yellowstone National Park. I stand in the woods, a stream behind me, a pair of heavy waders strapped over each shoulder, baggy at the hips and waist. My plaid shirt sleeves are rolled up, my tanned arms bare to the elbow. My fishing vest is hung with gadgets. A piece of fleece on one shoulder is decorated with half a dozen flies. On my head is a gray felt hat, a goose feather in the band sticking out jauntily. Two long, blonde braids come down over my breasts. I am smiling, leaning slightly on one leg, my hands clasped in front of me. There is an innocence in my round, soft face. A look that says I am happy to be here, this is my place.

Years ago a college friend came to Salt Lake City to ski and to stay with us. My mother had placed the picture on a bookshelf in the living room. He looked at it, took it up in both hands to get a better view, and turning to me with a curious look in his face, as if he had only then realized something terribly important—he said, "It's you. This is you. It's perfect." For him, the picture stilled me, *dis*tilled me, represented me as I *really* am, as he saw me, as he wanted me to be. Fishergirl. It is a picture that I want to show friends, and a picture that I want to hide. When I look at it now, I feel like an impostor. Fishergirl. It is me, and it isn't me. It was me, and it wasn't me. It always has been me and will never be me.

It was my father who taught me how to fly fish. And it was I who eagerly learned, never imagining that later, as a grown woman, the teaching would begin to feel like a molding. Never imagining that Fishergirl would grow to eclipse me, throwing a shadow over the many selves I wanted to become. I want to know, how much of me is this fishing girl and how much of that fishing girl is only borrowed, made up and put on? How much of Fishergirl is a sacrifice to my father's dream of a daughter, to my friends' desires for an eccentric companion, and how much is my own choice, my own desire? I want to let go of Fishergirl, shed her like a delicate snaky skin and start all over, making her up again, all by myself, as I go along.

On the train I lie with my head on a small, white pillow against the window, my curled body rocking, rocking with the rhythm of the moving cars. Even nested like this, I am restless. As always, I am disturbed by going home to the West, if not on the surface, then in the depths. It is only partly the severe landscape, the rocky dry March. I am agitated in the flesh-and-bone home of my body. The lost feeling started way back when the train left Chicago and is worse now. I get up and move through the train cars, descending to the lower level, furtively opening a window wide enough to feel fresh air on my face.

In transit, between one life and another, I forget who I am. I suffer again from an inexplicable loathing. "Let me out of this body," a voice inside me growls. My soul wants to take flight before we reach my destination. For a moment it is all I can do to stop from tearing myself limb from limb. In the train restroom, I wash my hands and face, lingering over my cheek bones as I dry them. "You," I say to myself in the mirror, "You are a pretty girl. Remember who you are." I look at my breasts, rounded under a rumpled blue T-shirt, my nipples showing through the thin cotton. I feel them being touched, gently by a woman I love. I remember that I am loved. I remember that this is one of the beautiful and distinctive things about a woman, her breasts. Slowly, I come back into myself.

When I return to my seat I pull from my red backpack a book my friend Cate gave me, *The River Why* by David James Duncan. It is a book about fishing for people who don't fish. Such books abound. For Father's Day one year I sent my father a copy of Norman Maclean's *A River Runs Through It.* My father and I exchanged letters about the book. He liked it but was tired of books that pretended to be about fishing and were really about politics or love instead. Once he visited me in St. Paul and on my shelf found a copy of Richard Brautigan's *Trout Fishing in America,* a bawdy, political book about love and sex and fly fishing; a commentary on the quality of life in America and how we treat nature. He looked through a couple of pages and said to me, almost angrily, "This isn't about fishing. This is crap."

I told him, "See, Trout Fishing in America is a guy, a man. It's a spoof on the myth and ideal of trout fishing." When Brautigan goes trout fishing he feels like a telephone repairman. He catches grotesque fish, not beautiful gleaming ones, but fish with ugly tumors and eyes half hanging out.

"It's supposed to be funny and ironic," I said again.

"I haven't seen anything funny yet," he said, shutting the book, putting Brautigan back on the shelf.

I open *The River Why* and start to read. Cate had given it to me nearly a year earlier, soon after we had met. Inside the front cover she wrote in the lovely and difficult-to-decipher script that still amuses me, "Gretchen—About fishing and love and other matters of the heart—With Great Affection this Easter Day, 1993." We had known each other only a month. We had never been fishing together. We had only watched movies and talked, eaten at restaurants, browsed antique stores. She had never seen me with a fishing pole in my hand. She had never seen me in a pair of waders. On our first date I dressed in a black leather miniskirt and jacket. Underneath I wore black fishnet pantyhose and a white nearly transparent tank top. My hair was freshly cut, clean on the back and sides and long enough on top to stand straight up. I waited for her on the sidewalk outside the restaurant, leaning with studied casualness against the brick of the building, my eyes shaded by sunglasses. When she arrived she daringly kissed me on the mouth in front of passing cars and couples strolling by.

After our date she gave me a note with a chocolate trout attached. The note said, "For Gretchen T. Legler, Fishergirl." The chocolate trout was covered in gaudy, bright foil. The note went on: "You are such a work. So rugged and graceful and raw and polished and pure. You are like a river through me. Everything seems fluid and everything possible." Already to her, even then, despite my leather miniskirt, despite the shades, despite my urban *machisma*, I was Fishergirl. She too was imagining me this way from the very beginning. How is it, I want to know, that we become who we are in other people's minds, and exactly how true are their visions of us? Who invented Fishergirl, and why does she stay with me?

Cate loved one specific part of the book and had marked it for me—a poem by William Butler Yeats, "The Song of Wandering Aengus." The poem for me is about many things, but mostly about desire—the pursuit of a vision of oneself, the pursuit of the *possibility* of self, of joy. It goes like this:

> *I went out to the hazel wood,*
> *Because a fire was in my head,*
> *And cut and peeled a hazel wand,*
> *And hooked a berry on a thread;*
> *And when white moths were on the wing,*
> *And moth-like stars were flickering out,*
> *I dropped the berry in the stream*
> *And caught a little silver trout.*
>
> *When I had laid it on the floor*
> *I went to blow the fire aflame,*
> *But something rustled on the floor,*
> *And some one called me by my name:*
> *It had become a glimmering girl*
> *With apple blossoms in her hair*
> *Who called me by my name and ran*
> *And faded through the brightening air.*
>
> *Though I am old with wandering*
> *Through hollow lands and hilly lands,*
> *I will find out where she has gone,*

And kiss her lips, and take her hands,
And walk along long dappled grass,
And pluck till time and times are done,
The silver apples of the moon,
The golden apples of the sun.

 The River Why is about a fishing family made up of Mister fly fisherman himself, Henning Hale-Orviston; Ma, an inveterate bait angler; and their sons Gus and Bill Bob, both of whom suffer minor emotional problems and act out rebelliously as a result of their parents' constant dueling over the relative merits of bait and flies. Henning, you see, wants his son Gus to be a fly fisherman. Ma, on the other hand, wants her son to catch as many fish as possible on the crudest of baits. She is happiest when he catches a record bass on a rotten wiener. The book is not really about fishing at all, but a setting for a story about love and spirituality and finding your own way in life—finding a way that is your own, finding a path that is not any path anyone has expected for you, laid for you or mapped for you. It is about finding out who you are. Who you are. Who you are. Who you are.

The train is making its way through a canyon along the Green River in Colorado. Hit now with late afternoon sun, the steep rocky walls are golden. As I try to read, I also listen to a family in the seats across from me. There is a little boy and a little girl. The parents are young and attractive. They laugh, they look each other in the eye, wink at each other and consult often about what they should do or will do or just did with the kids. "Case and I are going to the potty," the father says, as they head off down the stairs hand in hand. The little girl is standing up on his seat looking out the window. The mother says, "It's pretty out there, isn't it, with the sun on the rocks?" The little girl says, "Yes, and the river is pretty, too." I look out and see a fly fisherman, knee-deep in the river, and a naked man, lolling in a tiny tub made with rocks to hold a steaming hot spring. Both the fly fisher and the bather are waving up at us.

My mother is at the train station waiting for me, nervously scanning the train windows, watching the passengers getting off. But I make it across the platform and have her in my arms before she sees me. I am struck again by how small she feels, even wrapped in a sweater and parka against the late spring night. I am small, too, but feel beefy and huge compared to her.

It is well after midnight as we drive up from the valley and toward the mountains, toward Mt. Olympus, at the base of which my parents' house nearly lies. In my mother's kitchen, around the table, the room lit by the white light of the stove top, we talk. We lean close to one another and nearly whisper so as not to disturb my father, who was not up to greet me, but is sleeping in the basement in my brothers' old room. My mother reminds me not to flush the toilet upstairs because it will wake my father.

She tells me she has started doing something called container gardening. She points to two pots on the table, full of tiny plants. She is always starting something new, always following a new lead. She doesn't let herself get in a rut, become defined by the thing that she does. Once I finally got used to the idea of saying "My mother is a potter," she stopped making pots. Now she does container gardening, watches birds and grows herbs and roses. She has finally grown a perfect rose, she tells me. So perfect, so deep red, so velvety was this Lincoln Rose, that she brought it to work to show it off. "It may never happen again," she says. "I had to show it to someone."

The day before we leave for our trip, my mother and I shop and pack. Not only are we shopping for ourselves, but my mother is trying to get the house in order for my father as well. She has gone to three grocery stores, all far away from one another, to purchase his favorite muffins, biodegradable toilet paper and canned spaghetti with meat. She buys carrots and celery and cuts all the vegetables into thin strips and puts them in small Ziploc bags for his lunches. Then, she makes lasagna for our dinner. During a normal week she will do all of this and spend eight hours a day working as a secretary. My mother's life makes me tired. She is sixty-three years old.

My father wants to spend time with me on this morning before we leave. First, he talks to me about his computer, his "PowerBook," how it is the best computer he's ever bought and I should consider buying one, too. He then takes me on a tour of his new inventions. "Here," he says, "is my snowmelter for the cabin." It is a big garbage can with a brass faucet pushed into the side. He opens the back of his truck to show me his new winch. He shows me his bicycles. I feel as if I am watching a kid open toys at Christmas. He asks me if I would like to ride to the store with him to get some glue. I say, "No, Mom and I have things to pack yet," and he turns away from me gloomily.

Between packing and shopping, I wander around my parents' house, as I always do when I am home, looking to see what is new and what is still the same as it always was. I open the door to my father's office. Once it really was an office, piled with paper and books, but long ago it was turned into a fly-tying and rod-building room. Now the room has an eerie abandoned feel, as if he got up one day and walked away from it, leaving all these arti-facts behind. When my parents bought a piece of land on the Madison River in Montana, my father stopped fishing so much. He stopped tying flies and became obsessed, instead, with build-ing a cabin. His interests now are focused on composting toilets, solar power, battery banks and wells. He is the first president of the Landowners' Association and spends much of his time me-diating disputes among the city slickers who, like him, bought thirty-acre parcels of the subdivided ranch their property is part of.

My mother warned me about the office. "I don't like to go in there," she said. "I think there may be black widows in the cor-ners." When I open the door a smell rich and thick meets my nose—a smell of the skins of birds and old, old smoke. The walls are still thickly covered with plastic bags of fly-tying material hanging from hooks; peacock herl, rabbit fur, skins of mallards and wooducks, tinsel and bright yarn, packages of turkey quills, pheasant necks, swatches of deer hair. The shelves are lined with tidy chests containing pullout boxes of hooks, bottles of glue, tweezers and other small tools. Several fly-tying vises still are clamped to the edge of the desk. And from every surface sprout flies—elaborate streamers, tiny imitation mosquitoes, deer-hair grasshoppers of varying sizes, scrubby-looking nymphs and ele-gant Royal Coachmans.

He had tried to teach me to tie flies. He gave me a book on fly tying for Christmas one year: *Jack Dennis' Western Trout Fly-Tying Manual.* Inside the cover it was inscribed "To Gretty from Daddy, Christmas 1986. I hope you will find this as useful as I did. You must still learn the basics first." I was twenty-six then. I never learned even the basics. The flies I did tie have all unraveled in my fly box.

That night around the dinner table it's mostly my father talking and me listening. My mother is quietly eating, sipping icy tonic water from a tall glass. She gets up and serves my father more lasagna when he asks for it. He talks about being close to retiring from his job as a professor and how university people are hovering, like vultures, waiting to move in on his space. He feels angry. He has worked hard and wants to be respected. It isn't fair, and I tell him so. In these rare moments when despite everything I see his fear, my heart opens to him. But it never stays open long—long enough, that is, to make anything change.

Still later, after we have spent some time talking about how I will be moving to Alaska soon, my father clears his throat and says, "I'd like to come up there and fish with you." A tiny, cramped part of my heart smirks. Fat chance, I think. I am moving to a new place, with a chance to start all over, a new life, and already he wants to come and fish with me. Already I am going there to be Fishergirl. What about the rest of it, I want to ask him. I am also going to Alaska to work, to start my first job as a professor of English and creative writing. I will be a teacher, like him. A writer. A member of a new community. I will be meeting people, dating, buying a home, maybe even building a log cabin. I will be so much more and other than Fishergirl. I want to smother my own desire to be Fishergirl and even suffer the damage I do to myself in the process, all to finally wreck this rickety bridge that joins us, to wipe away this part of me that feels so made by him.

∽

We started out fishing as a family, my two brothers, my sister and I, my mother and my father. At first we fished from a small aluminum boat at big artificial lakes around Salt Lake— Strawberry Reservoir, Deer Creek. We fished for trout and perch, trolling big red and white lures. Or we fished from shore with worms and corn. We made jigs in the basement, pouring hot lead into tiny molds, then dressing up the jigs with black and yellow feathers. In the beginning we had trout in the freezer. We had trout for breakfast. We had trout in the sink, still wet and gleaming, just taken off the stringer. For years we fished this way.

Then things began to change, and we didn't have so much fish around anymore. Fishing became more about art than food. Both of my parents became interested in fly fishing. It was my mother who started tying flies, ordering great quantities of feathers and thread and vises and scissors and glue from *Herter's* magazine. At first we still used spinning reels, attaching the flies to lines rigged with water-filled clear bubbles so that we could cast them out far into the mountain lakes we backpacked to.

Gradually fishing in our family became more and more specialized, until tying flies and building rods became my father's hobby. My father took a special interest in teaching me to fly fish. For me, as a teenager, it was something romantic and different. I made a transition, a leap into a new identity, that summer at Yellowstone, the summer my brother took the picture of me— I changed from a silly, ordinary girl with no boyfriends and straight A's on my report card into Fishergirl. The fishing will never be as good for me as it was that summer.

My father would walk with me to the stream edge, pointing

to pools where he said he knew there were fish. He showed me how to cast, keeping my fly line up in the air, throwing out enough line to get my fly to the shaded, cool bank on the opposite side. Then he would leave me to fish alone.

I caught cutthroat after cutthroat, moving slowly down the stream, fishing the big pools and the noisy shallow riffles, too. Sun warmed the back of my neck, the air was dense with the sound of snapping grasshoppers and the smell of sage and pine, all mixed with the coolness rising up from the stream. Nothing then could have done me any harm. When I'd caught so many fish that my imitation grasshopper was frayed, I changed to something colorful and big. I didn't know the names, and I wasn't picky. I'd cast the fly upstream and watch its big wings float quickly down, my body tensed for the sight of a swirl, the popping sound of a trout's lips pulling my fly down into the water. Once, a voice startled me, "You're a natural, you know," and I turned around to find my father sitting on the gravel, his back against the cutbank, smoking a cigarette and watching me. "Do you like this?" he asked me then. I told him there was no place else in the world I would rather be.

The morning my mother and I finally leave for our road trip, my father is sitting in the kitchen with his portable computer and Post-it notes and pens of different colors. He props the computer up next to his cereal bowl and works. My mother reminds me he needs to be where it is light and cheery. He needs the sun, she says, or he gets depressed. But it means there is no room for her. She finally told him, she says, not to put his stuff out on weekend mornings when she is home. He does it anyway, and when she comes in he says, "Do you want me to move now?"

We tell him we're going to leave at 7:00 A.M. "Maybe you will, maybe you won't," he says crossly. I am finishing my last cup of coffee before we get in the car. My father and I are standing at the kitchen window, looking out at their cat, Bilbo, who is sitting awkwardly, one arthritic leg sticking out at a right angle, in a shaft of dusty sunshine on the balcony.

He asks me if I know how old Bilbo is. I say no, I can't remember when we got her. He looks me in the eye and says soberly, "Bilbo is twenty years old." I am appropriately amazed.

"She doesn't do much anymore," he says. "She likes to sit in the sun and sleep mostly. She's slowing down." He seems saddened by this, but also comforted, as if the cat is doing just exactly what an old cat, or an old person, should be doing—slowing down, enjoying what he or she loves best. The conversation makes me wonder about my father, about my mother, about how much time I have left with my parents. I guess, twenty years, maybe. That's only a handful. I can imagine these years with my mother, but no clear picture of the woman I am now comes to me with my father in it.

I became my father's fishing pal. Some mornings I would be awakened so early that I cried as I tied my bootlaces, not wanting to go on yet another fishing trip, not wanting to go out into the cold morning. But later, on the water, as we motored through thick fog, and when I brought home a twenty-inch rainbow trout with a story about how it grabbed my red and white Dare-Devil when the lure had just hit the water, I felt sure that this was who I was. Fishergirl. When I was older we would go on Sunday trips, sometimes with my brother, Austin, but many times alone. We would drive up out of Salt Lake, past Park City, into the mountains to fish shallow, rocky streams.

Somehow we became locked into a vision of one another as Fishergirl and her dad. I knew hardly anything else about him except this. For Father's Day I would send him woodduck skins, or trout napkins, or mugs with fish for handles. For Christmas he gave me boxes of leader material, little leather envelopes with sheep fleece linings for storing flies, small scissors attached to re-tractable cords for clipping fly line while standing up to your waist in water. One Christmas I opened package after package of fly fishing gadgets. There was a zippered leather envelope full of half a dozen dazzling streamers, a brooch made out of a huge and elaborate fly, a mobile of a trout and flies, a little pad of fly line cleaner, a spool of fly line. Mary, my brother's girlfriend, handed me another package, this one wrapped in lavender and tied with a turquoise bow. She winked at me. "This is for you, Gretty, be-cause you're a woman, too." Inside the box was a bar of scented soap, body powder and bath oil. Mary winked at me again, as if to say, he sometimes forgets.

When my mother and I leave at 7:00 A.M., my father is in the shower where he can't possibly say good-bye. He went there as we were heading out the door. I want him to be different. I want him to help us carry out our bags, to help load them into the car, to hug us each good-bye and kiss us on the cheek, to wish us good luck and good fun and to stand in the driveway and wave as we drive off into the morning. This may never happen. I can't depend on his changing.

Five hours later, my mother and I arrive at Hovenweep, our first stop. We walk down into a shaded valley, perfumed with sand dust and sage. The bluffs above the valley are ringed with dilapidated sandstone houses, put together brick by brick centuries ago. My mother needs to stop often. Her doctors won't treat her cough, she says, with some amount of anger. They just tell her to quit smoking. This walking is hard on her, but we go at her pace and I am in no hurry. We spend our first night at a hotel owned by a German woman and her husband in Cortez, Colorado. We get a message at the desk that someone has called for us. It was my father. We left an explicit itinerary with phone numbers so he knows exactly where we are. My mother calls home, and my father wants to know where the cat food is for Bilbo.

On the second day we go to the Four Corners and take goofy pictures. In one I am doing a Twister pose with my hands and feet in all four states and my mother's shadow is cast across me. At the Four Corners we both buy jewelry. My mother is gracious and kind to the Navajo women artists. She made pots for so long, and for so long sold them for not even half of the work she put into them. She knows how hard this kind of work is. "I love your work," she tells the women, and she smiles.

Before we go to Mesa Verde we visit the Anasazi Heritage Center. As we walk around the center, she coughs. I go from exhibit to exhibit looking at baskets under glass, a whole pithouse reassembled, panoramas, diagrams, collections of arrowheads and artists' reconstructions of pueblo life. As I walk I hear her cough echo through the museum.

At Mesa Verde, we walk down to Spruce House. We are guided by a ranger who doesn't lie to us. He reminds me of Burl Ives—he has red hair and a red beard, a big belly and a deep, friendly voice. His story about the ancient people is full of holes. "We really don't know exactly why they built in this canyon," he says. "Some people say for protection against marauding enemies. But you know, that's a particular idea that may be more about us than about them. These are only educated guesses." He asks us to speculate about the tiny houses built up in the thin wedges in the cliff. "Privacy," someone says. "Lookouts," someone else says. He smiles and suggests that in such close quarters maybe lovers used these huts as places to be together. This idea appeals to me.

At the visitors' center I buy a book called *Our Trip to Mesa Verde, 1922*, a chronicle of four girls' trip to Mesa Verde. The girls, who were friends and school teachers, hiked the whole way from Ouray, Colorado, to Mesa Verde and back, to see the cliff houses that were just then being excavated and opened to the public. Ruth E., Ruth H., Dot and Fetzie were their names. How unordinary they must have been, four girls alone, hiking through the sage, in 1922. I envy them their bravery. I want to be like that. In the pictures they look wonderful and flamboyant in tall lace-up boots and dusty trousers, floppy hats and old-fashioned packs. The trip took them a month. In the epilogue, written in 1988, Ruth E. writes that each one of them married and they all lived happily ever after.

At the hotel in Durango, Colorado, we joke with the two young women who are behind the desk. They are tanned and clear-faced with perfect teeth and wide mouths. Their eyes are bright. My mother asks if there have been any phone calls for us. I joke that we're on the run. "Thelma and Louise," my mother says, smiling at them and winking. The girls laugh. For dinner we eat at an Italian restaurant. For dessert my mother has custard with raspberry cordial sauce and wants the recipe from the waiter. She vows when we get home she will buy a cookbook to reproduce this dessert.

While we are getting ready for bed, my mother tells me that her arthritis is so bad now she can hardly pull on her pantyhose anymore. But, she says wryly, "The good thing about getting old is learning to accept yourself." I keep seeing her in a picture from long ago when she used to be a model. In the picture she wears a black short skirt and waist jacket and a black pillbox hat. For a time, when we were young, my mother tried to teach my sister, Ally, and me how to be ladies. She bought us each a pair of white gloves. She taught us how to roll on pantyhose. "Always wear your gloves when you put on your hose," she said, "or you'll put runs in them." Ally and I walked around the living room with books balanced on our heads, practicing good posture. She wanted me to learn to walk with my feet straight, not sticking out to the sides like a duck. She showed us how to turn, like models on a fashion runway.

Most weekends, when I was young, we went fishing. We would drive through mountain valleys, and at every bridge or roadside rest, my father would get out and look at the water. Mostly we were all bored silly, fidgeting in the back seat of the car. But there was also a part of me that paid attention when he would stop the car on the side of the road, walk over to the streamside or look down on it from the bridge, and come back with a report. "Seems high," he'd say. At the next one he'd stop the car, get out, come back, "Seems muddy," he'd say. And again, "Looks clear."

This is one of the reasons I signed on as Fishergirl in the first place. I wanted to be like this—to be interested in and knowledgeable about one thing. His love of streams, of fishing, seemed so complete and pure and mysterious. He knew something we didn't, and I wanted to know what it was. I wanted to learn how to find fish, how to tell a good stream from a bad one, how not to frighten a trout in the water, what fly to use. Mostly I wanted to know what it was that he loved so much. I wanted to experience that, too, to love something so utterly you assumed everyone else was as fascinated with it as you.

I took my fly rods with me to college. I had two, both safely traveling in black plastic tubes, with my name on them in gold tape. My father had made both of the rods and the carrying tubes for me. I stored the rods in my dorm room, in the back of the closet. No one I knew at college wanted to fish. But they all liked the idea that I had fly rods in the back of my closet. It made me interesting. A professor of mine flattered me by giving me a fly-tying kit—a big metal box filled with clear plastic drawers. In each drawer was something new—hooks of different sizes, colored thread and tinsel, feathers, hair, yarn and glue. He had bought it thinking he'd get into fly fishing, he said. But he had never opened it. I have moved the kit around with me to six different homes and apartments. I've never used it either.

One weekend in college I could not bear the city a moment longer and headed off to the rolling green hills of southern Minnesota to fish. I did some research and got the trout stream maps from the Minnesota Department of Natural Resources. I thought I knew exactly where I was going. As I drove along the dirt roads in the hot and heavy humid air, I slowly passed a black Amish buggy. Two little boys in flat straw hats grinned and waved at me. Their father, driving, nodded as I passed them. I was proud and feeling independent, feeling like Fishergirl.

I drove around all day looking for the stream that looked just right—something wide and deep, like the streams in Utah and Wyoming. But these streams confused me. They were all thin and muddy and covered over by trees. How would you fish a stream like this? A kind of indecision had seized me. Alone I realized that this was no fun at all. The whole activity lost its meaning. I drove back to the city, to my dorm room and my books. I had not even wetted my line. I felt somehow stupid and false, as if I wasn't cut out for this at all, as if without my father by my side, I was no Fishergirl at all. I wanted to be solid unto myself and, instead, I felt full of holes.

When my mother and I leave Durango, we head off in the wrong direction. All the while we are driving happily and talking. We talk about her pottery. She tries to explain to me that the pots themselves were never her goal. That the whole thing was about process. And when she stopped making pots, it wasn't as if she had stopped being herself. She just moved on to something new. Pottery defined her for me for so long. She was always in the garage working with a mound of clay on her wheel, loading her kiln, or in the kitchen with a pot on the table, rubbing the outside with a wooden spoon to make it shine. Her pots were mostly hand-built. She was trying, she said, to replicate Anasazi methods and designs. There was always clay on the doorknobs, clay on the phone.

Now she's stopped. She tells me that my father keeps asking her when she'll get back to pottery. "Maybe never," she tells him. She says to him, "I'm just not interested anymore." Now the garage is full of his tools and gadgets, and the kiln is on the back porch under a tarp. "What do you mean you're not interested anymore?" he asks her. She tells him that she is changing, that's it, and that he has changed, too; after all, he quit tying flies.

~

My mother and I get to Silverton before I realize we are going the wrong way. I tell her sheepishly that we need to turn around. She heads back up over the pass on the curving road we've just come down. It is cold on top of the pass. There is a lot of snow. It is beautiful. She tells me that she dreams about being on an endless road and coming to crevasse after crevasse and turning around. "This has something to do with life," she says, her eyes on the road, both hands on the wheel.

We talk about my being a lesbian. She tells me that since I told her this about myself she has discovered that everywhere she turns there is a lesbian or a gay man—an author, a friend, a movie star and ordinary people, too. The letter I wrote to my parents, in which I revealed the reason I had left my husband, was boring and full of platitudes. It was full of short, declarative sentences. I had been careful with every word, every phrase. I wanted them both to understand plainly, with no flourishes, what had happened to me, how I had changed, how I had emerged. The letter had nothing in it of the joy I felt at the time. I was unaccustomed to the language of joy. The very word "joy" felt awkward in my hands. I had hardly a vocabulary to express myself, whereas I had practiced for years the language of grief. "I am so happy," I told my parents in the letter. That is the word I repeated over and over and over. Happy. Happy. Happy. Only my mother understood. She turns to me now in the car and says, "You seem happier."

My mother telephoned as soon as she got my letter. I was sitting at the kitchen table by an open window. There was sun shining in. Cate sat next to me in a chair, holding my hand with both of hers. My mother did not say much. I had to chip loose what I wanted from her. I asked, "Are you surprised?"

"Yes and no."

"Are you sad?"

"Yes."

"Why?"

"The world is so unpredictable. Things hardly ever go any- more as you expect."

I was quiet.

"I have been thinking about how much it takes to raise a child," she said. "And I think we always did the right thing, but maybe not." She paused and then said, "I know we always did stop for ice cream."

Afterward, exhausted, I lay down in bed next to Cate and we slept. It had been easier than I had imagined, telling my mother. She had said all of the right things. "We still love you," she had said. But still, I was overcome by a deep weariness all mixed up with sadness and a clear sense of being suddenly released from a great, sagging weight. I was free. Free. Free of something. What? Free to do what? Be what? In my sleep I dreamed of my sister, Ally. I dreamed I was holding her hand, and I woke with Cate's hand in mine. I slept again, and awoke when I heard someone call me by my name. "Gretchen," the voice said. Only once. And very clear. Again, Cate was sound asleep beside me.

As my mother drives, I ask her why my father never called me about the letter. "I'll tell you, but you won't like it," she says. "He said he didn't care as long you didn't tell everybody. He thinks sexual proclivities are private things."

"Oh," I say.

"And he never read your letter."

My heart lands like a stone in my chest.

"He worries about you," she tells me, "that it will be hard for you to be happy like this. That it will be hard for you to get a job." I laugh. My life has never been this easy. I have finally claimed space for myself against the forces that work to keep us all from knowing who we are; the forces that keep us pasting ourselves together from the fragments of other people's desires. Of course, I think, he would never read my letter. He wouldn't understand it, and it would frighten him.

There is another picture of me fly fishing. This time in color, taken by Craig when we were still married. In it I am wearing a bright-red flannel shirt. On my head is the same old hat, adorned with a different feather—still long and gray, something I picked up along a stream or in the woods, vowing that I'd place it in my hat and never forget where it came from. My fly rod is tucked under one arm, and in my other hand I am holding a shining, flickering cutthroat trout upside down by the tail. I learned all this from my father. When you get the fish, you pull in line enough so you have the fish under control; then you pull your bandanna from your vest, wet it, and taking the fish gently by its strong tail, lift it out of the water and carefully take the fly out of its mouth. Before you had even started to fish, you had clipped the barb off of the hook so that the fish's mouth would be hurt as little as possible. Then you let the fish go, first holding it by its tail in the stream until it has got its wits back and can swim away.

On the day this picture was taken, Craig caught an extraordinary fish. We had seen it lurking in the shade under the opposite bank, and Craig worked all morning to get it to strike. He played the fish too long, however, and by the time it was unhooked the fish was frail. And when he released it, the fish turned over on its back, its white belly open to the sky. Craig was cradling it in his palms in the water when my father appeared around the bend. He showed Craig how to resuscitate a fish by moving it slowly back and forth in the water, forcing oxygen into its gills. He did this with his big, intelligent hands until the fish flipped its tail and swam strongly upstream. Craig told me, jokingly, that he was lucky. He only caught fish when my father was there to see it. He seemed to understand so quickly something I had painfully felt all of my life, that being good at fishing somehow wins my father's respect.

On one of our first dates, I took Craig to Hay Creek, a tiny trout stream in southern Minnesota. I wanted to impress Craig, so in preparation for the trip I called my father for advice. I told him that I didn't know how to fish these little Minnesota streams, and he told me I should use wet flies. Nymphs. He sent me a gift of a small packet of fluorescent green and orange "strike indicators," bits of colored foam tape you tear off and stick on your leader when you are using a nymph. You watch the strike indicator and when it stops moving, odds are your nymph is being nibbled by a trout. I hear his voice, "My nymph fishing improved about fifty percent when I started using strike indicators."

On that trip, Craig and I fished in ankle-deep water, catching two small trout; then we spread out a blanket beside the stream for our lunch. We played, putting grapes in each other's mouths, feeding each other sliced apples and cheese, and then started to kiss, finally making slow love in the tall grass. I saw sky over his back. I heard birds and the water. I smelled warm dust from the road. We washed naked in the cold stream, and I teased him that this was a risky idea he had had, what with the road so near. "It was your idea too," he said, smiling.

Craig took a picture of me on that trip that he later had a friend of ours make into a watercolor painting. I often think that it is only partly an image of me that emerged on that photographic paper; the rest is Craig's vision of me, fed by his love. The painting hung above our bed, until after we divorced and Craig gave it back to me—my shining face and blue, blue eyes, a green shirt, a green hat and a yellow daisy in the hatband. In the painting, I look like a wood sprite. I look like Fishergirl.

My mother and I are winding our way toward Chaco Canyon on the third day of our trip. We take a thin, rutted dirt road, so narrow in places and hemmed in by red rock that I wonder if the car will fit through. It is early in the season and the road hasn't been graded yet. All the ruins here are in the canyon bottom, not up in the cliffs. Pueblo Bonito, the largest ruin in the canyon, is said to have been a mecca, a cultural and political center, crawling with people, surrounded by farms. There are roads carved in the sandstone, going up over the red rock sides of the canyon and leading to other pueblos. One story is that Pueblo Bonito got too large. There were a couple of bad years. Everyone died or moved. I want to know where the people went. I want to know what happened to their lives, their individual, private lives.

I tell my mother I am finally beginning to figure out my life. I am realizing that there are doors that will not always be open to me. I feel as if I am becoming wise, that my youth is ending. She looks at me and says quietly, "People talk about finding the meaning of life. People used to know what the meaning of life was—a job and a place to live and enough to eat. Life has gotten so complicated."

We talk about my father. She tells me that before my visit,

my father asked especially for her to sit and talk to him about something important. They sat, one on each end of the kitchen table, and he told her that he was worried about my visit. He was worried that I would be difficult. Difficult. I would ask hard questions. I would rebel in small, insignificant ways. I would frustrate him by sleeping in late, waking only after he had left the house, by staying up late, talking with my mother in the kitchen long after he had gone to bed, and by crying. "He always makes you cry," my mother has said on other visits. "I hope he doesn't make you cry. You don't have to let him make you cry."

My mother tells me that my father wants to spend time with me. "He wants to spend time with you *alone*," she says. "He tells me that he hasn't spent time with you alone in three years." Alone for what, I want to ask. Even when we are alone together, the space between us is like a vast canyon that our voices barely carry across. The last time we were alone together, we went fishing at my parents' cabin in Montana. We packed lunches and water and hiked down the steep slope to the Madison River. As we put on our wading gear and tied on flies, he talked to me about my mother. He said he loved her and didn't want her to die before he did.

"Have you told her that?" I asked.

"Not in so many words," he said. "There's no doubt in my mind. Unless I get hit by a car, I will outlive your mother."

He left me at the first pool. I watched him tromping downstream in his waders and fishing vest, his rod tip bobbing as he stepped over grassy hummocks, until he disappeared around the first big bend. I tied on a fly, something big with white wings that I could see easily in the fast water, and listlessly cast out and drew in line for two hours. My father, I knew, would be catching fish. He would be taking up netfuls of river water, scientifically determining the insects the fish were eating, and then finding (or tying) an exact match.

When he came back to join me at lunch time, he found me lying in the sun, reading a mystery novel. Beside me I had a stack of reeds I had collected for my mother, who wanted them to thatch the roofs of the birdhouses my father had been building from hollowed-out logs. He set his rod down in the grass and took a sip of water. He asked me, "Have you ever thought we were rich?" I said no. "Well, we're not rich. We never have been. But Mother has done an incredible job managing our finances, so we have a good ratio of income to outflow and a good retirement." I asked if he had told her that. "Not in so many words," he said. "I'm tempted to ask her to show me how to do it. I'm going to need to know." I want to ask him with what words or what actions he *has* told her that he loves her. I want to ask him if he loves me.

On the fourth day my mother and I leave Gallup and go to Window Rock on the Navajo Reservation. We stop at the Hubbell Trading Post and visit a shop where Navajo women are weaving. My mother wants to talk to them, but they only smile at her. She looks to a young woman and says to her, "I guess I don't speak their language. Can you ask them how long it takes them to weave one of these rugs?" The young woman says something to the older women, and then turns to my mother and says, "These are women in their seventies. They only speak *Dine*. They never went to school. They were old-fashioned and stayed home all of their lives, you know. It takes them hundreds of

hours to weave a blanket." When we leave, my mother thanks
the old weavers and the young woman who was her interpreter.
My mother is one of the nicest people I know.

In the beginning I liked that fly fishing with my father made me
feel somehow superior to people who fished with spinning gear
and bait. I felt as if I had evolved into a more refined and more
intelligent creature when I learned to fly fish. I would laugh at
the jokes my father would make about hayseeds who fished with
corn and cheeseballs. But after a while the jokes didn't seem
funny anymore. On one particular trip I remember feeling
ashamed and putting the shame in my pocket like a shell or a
tiny pinecone.

My father and brother and I had set out on an already hot,
dry morning for the lower part of Slough Creek in Yellowstone.
We had taken a short cut over a steep hill, into the woods, where
we often saw moose and deer. Far away, up higher on the green
meadows, we had heard elk bugle. Along the way we had met a
horse-drawn wagon taking this route to a dude ranch north of
the park. We got to the stream, and there was no one there yet.
As we sat on a log by the very first pool, quiet at that time of day,
still and amber-colored, we peeled off our boots and wool socks
and put on waders and wading shoes and got our fly rods set. I
was missing something, as always, and had to ask for it—some
tippet, some leader, maybe a few extra flies. My father handed
them over impatiently, as if to say, you're old enough now to
have your fishing vest in order.

As we were preparing to fish, a father and son arrived, talking loudly, breaking the still. And my father muttered under his
voice as they moved away, walking merrily along the high grassy

bank, that they would scare the fish, that they shouldn't be allowed here with their spinning gear and flashing, hook-heavy
lures. I told him in the kind of controlled, angry voice in which I
was learning to speak with him, "It isn't our stream." He looked
at me and smiled and said, "Yes, it is." Instead of feeling fine and
laughing, I just felt snobbish, and I knew it wasn't right.

We are headed to Canyon de Chelly. My mother describes a
movie to me about a woman and man who fall in love. He's an
ex-con. The man and woman kiss in the movie. It is their first
kiss, tentative and full of passion. She could feel the passion, she
says, the electricity. She hasn't felt that way in a long time.

"Is that what you feel?" she asks me, tentatively.

"You mean with a woman?"

"Yes," she says.

"Yes," I answer. "Now more than ever before." I try to explain this to her. "It wasn't that I never had great sex with men,"
I say. "It's that with them, with men, I was never fully present in
my own body." She tells me that she is surprised and a little em-
barassed that I talk so easily about sex.

At Canyon de Chelly we walk down into the wash to see the
White House Ruins. I keep handing my mother my water bottle
and urging her to drink. "Water is good for you," I say. It is a
steep walk, and she goes slowly. At the bottom there is thin
spring grass and a hogan, and red walls rising up to blue cloudless
sky. We walk along the wash in the deep sand to the ruins, where
there are other people who have come down in four-wheel-drive
vehicles with Navajo guides.

At the ruins some women have spread out blankets and are
selling jewelry. I buy a silver medallion, shaped like the sun, on a

leather string. Coming up from the bottom of the canyon, my mother takes a picture of me in my bluejeans and ribbed, sleeveless undershirt, the medallion around my neck. In the picture I imagine coming from this shot, I look hot and tanned. I am smiling. My breasts show rounded under my shirt. This will be a sexy picture. Cate will like this, I think. I have never felt this way about my body before—recognizing it as desirable. It is the same body I have always had, but I am different in it now.

The last stop my mother and I make is in Kayenta, Arizona. As we drive there, night is coming on and the clouds above us turn slowly from pink to peach to gold. The clouds are so close and the color so intense that I feel as if we are rising up into them, as if we are flying, as if at any moment we will burst through this blanket of gold and be soaring among stars in a blue-black sky. At the hotel we have Navajo fry bread and salad for dinner. Just to watch her order from a menu, to see her make a choice about what it is that she wants, such a simple choice, gives me a feeling of great intimacy. Neither one of us sleeps well. Clearly, we don't want to go home.

As we drive through Monument Valley the next morning, the sun comes up deep burnt-orange behind the weird sandstone sculptures of the valley. My mother keeps saying to me that this is the best vacation she has ever had. "You're easy to be with," she says. She is surprised by the things I do for her, such as open doors and carry her suitcase. "You are so polite," she says.

When we get back to Salt Lake she wants to have our pictures developed right away. We drop them off at the camera counter at Safeway, even before we reach home, and rush back to get them exactly an hour later. We show them to my father. He looks at three or four and puts the stack aside.

72

⌐

There is another picture of me fly fishing. I am older still. Maybe thirty. I stand in a wide, curving stream with my fly rod, casting out into the silver water with dark trees rising behind me and gray-blue mountains beyond that. The picture looks romantic and perfect: girl and stream. Mountains. Fish. But I remember this time. I remember my heavy pack, the black flies biting at my neck, my Royal Humpy caught on the rocks and willows behind me. I remember not catching fish and wondering again why I was out there in the stream up to my thighs in water.

I remember, too, that there was then, and has been every time I have gone fishing with my father, a laughing in the water and the pleasant crunch of gravel under my boots and relief offered by the cool wafts of watery air that came up from the stream. There was the rich smell of fish and weeds and pebbles and muck from the undercut banks hung over with grass.

I remember, too, amid the peace and the real joy, a feeling of being trapped. I don't love this, I wanted to shout out so that my voice echoed off the mountains. I'll never love it like you do. Can't you see? I'm doing it for you, to be with you. I'm trying. And it isn't working.

My father agrees to take me to the train station at 5:00 A.M., long before my train is supposed to leave. Already he has been up for hours, typing on his computer at the breakfast table. He will go straight from the train station to his lab and work. He asks me if I will come and visit him at his cabin in Montana this summer. I tell him no. I can't spend time with him alone now, until something, anything, even something small, changes between us. He asks me what I would like for my graduation present and suggests some stocks that his parents gave him when he graduated with his Ph.D. in biology. In the secret, angry language that passes between us, I hear him saying that he loves me. I want him to say it out loud. I want him, out loud, to ask me something real about my life and to tell me something real about his.

Our strongest connection lies in fly fishing, but I want more than this—I want him to understand me in my wholeness. I want him to know what else there is about me besides Fishergirl. "You want me to fish with you," I want to say, "I want you to see who I am." And I want to tell him this, that I am an ordinary woman who is thirty-four years old and owns a stained, smelly fishing vest, only half of the pockets with anything in them at all. I am an ordinary woman with a crumpled and eclectic collection of flies, an unused fly-tying kit, two fly rods, two reels, some cracked nylon wading shoes, a pair of old-fashioned rubber waders and a couple of books on fly tying. And besides all of this, I have two cats. I like to drink strong coffee in the morning. I dance the two-step to country music. I own a leather miniskirt and purple cowboy boots. I love my crewcut hair. I sip chamomile tea every night before bed. I have gone canoeing in the wilderness alone. I won a medal in a cross-country ski race. I have ordinary desires, to love and be adored. Bills to pay. I am moving to Alaska. And I am a lesbian. He has no idea of who I am.

He hugs me awkwardly, and when I look at him tears are pooling in his eyes. After he leaves I sit in the waiting area and open *The River Why* again. In the last chapters—Gus goes off to a cabin in the woods to fish and be alone. Released finally from the pressing of both of his strong-willed parents—the fly fisher and the bait angler, Gus finds himself, and he finds his true love, a glimmering fishing girl with apple blossoms in her hair. In many ways he gives up on his family, gives up about them ever being different, and sets off to have a new life.

One day, upon returning to his cabin, Gus sees by the stream that runs in front of his house, an old man with a straw hat tipped over one eye, lounging in a chair and fishing with worms. He doesn't recognize the fellow and lets him be. Farther along the stream Gus sees an old woman elegantly decked out in tweeds, fly casting, perfectly. He doesn't recognize her either, but watches her for a while, impressed. Soon he begins to realize that he does know these two. He realizes that they are his mother and father and that they have changed.

When the train arrives I shut my book and move out into the darkness of the platform. I shove my bags aboard and settle into my seat, my face pressed against the window. The train doesn't move for a long time, and I drift off to sleep, dreaming. In the dream my mother is in her kitchen. She wants me to spend more time with my father. "He has something important to show you," she says. My father enters the kitchen, pale and thin, with red and tired eyes, but he is excited, like a boy, showing me his latest miraculous inventions—a new way to fasten rain gutters to the cabin roof, or this, a clip for attaching a cable to a battery, or this, blueprints for a straw tool shed. As I turn away from him, he collapses, folding to the floor like a dropped cloth, and I run to him calling "Daddy, Daddy, Daddy."

I am startled awake by the train lurching away from the platform with a deep metallic creak and a moan. My heart is pumping unevenly in my chest. I whisper to myself, the words coming out softly and making misty spots on the window glass near my face, "Is it time?" Is it all right to go ahead and admit that I am blood of his blood, that I am my father's daughter, that *this*, that loving to fish, is a gift, that we love some of the same things? In a moment so bright and quick that I hardly know what it is, I understand one thing—no one can do that to anyone else; no one can fix or freeze anyone else. It's just me who has felt unable to contradict the molding. The more I know who I am, the more I will be able to see who I am, I think, smiling to myself over how much of a riddle it sounds. I am, at least partly, and all on my own, Fishergirl. I am, I am, I am.

As we begin to move, to gather speed, something begins to gather in me—it comes slowly, then faster, then comes on all at once, like a river of heat rolling up from my toes, filling the hollowness of my body, making my scalp prickle, my fingers tremble. This is joy, this thing I was so unaccustomed to not so long ago. *I have changed.* I close my eyes and see a glimmering girl emerge from a silver trout, lithe and shining, running, calling, calling me, calling me by my name.

PAM HOUSTON

The Company of Men

I CAN'T REMEMBER the last time I envied a man, or, in fact, if I ever have. I have loved men, hated them, befriended them, taken care of them, and all too often compromised my sense of self for them, but I don't think I have ever looked at a man and actually coveted something his maleness gave him. And yet envy was at least one of the surprising things I felt last spring when I found myself standing armpit-deep in a freshwater stream at 2:00 A.M., near Interlochen, Michigan, fly casting for steelhead with a bunch of male poets.

Winters are long in northern Michigan, and dark and frozen.

Spring is late and wet and full of spirit-breaking storms. The landscape is primarily forest and water and has not been tamed like most of the Midwest. Both the wildness and the hardship show on the faces of the people who choose to live there.

When a man named Jack Driscoll first calls and invites me to Interlochen, he tells me about the Academy, a place where talented high-school students from forty-one states and fifteen countries are given a lot of time to develop their art. Although he makes it clear that I will be expected to read from my fiction and talk to the students about craft, every other time we speak on the phone, all he really wants to talk about is fishing.

For all the time I spend outdoors, I am not much of a fisherman. And fly fishing, like all religions, is something I respect but don't particularly understand. If Jack bothers to ask me if I want to go fishing, I will say yes. I have always said yes, and as a result the shape of my life has been a long series of man-inspired adventures, and I have gone tripping along behind those men, full of strength and will and only a half-baked kind of competence, my goal being not to excel, but to simply keep up with them, to not become a problem, to be a good sport. It is a childhood thing (I was my father's only son), and I laugh at all the places this particular insecurity has taken me: sheep hunting in Alaska, helicopter skiing in Montana, cliff diving in the Bahamas, ice climbing in the Yukon territory. Mostly, I have outgrown the need to impress men in this fashion; in the adventures I take these days, I make the rules. But, as my trip to Michigan draws nearer, I feel a familiar and demented excitement to be back at the mercy of a bunch of lunatic outdoorsmen, a stubborn novice with something intangible to prove.

I fly up to Traverse City on what the woman at the United Express counter calls the "big" plane, a twin-engine that bumps between thunderstorms and patches of dense fog for an hour before skidding to a stop on a bleak and rainy runway surrounded by a leafless April woods.

I am greeted by what looks like a small committee of fit and weathered middle-aged men. Their names are Jack Driscoll, Mike Delp, Nick Bozanic and Doug Stanton. Their books are titled after the landscape that dominates their lives, collections of poetry called *Under the Influence of Water*, *The Long Drive Home* and *Over the Graves of Horses*, and Jack's award-winning collection of stories titled *Wanting Only to Be Heard*. They fight over my luggage, hand me snacks and sodas and beers, and all but carry me to the car on the wave of their enthusiasm.

"Weather's been good," Mike says, by way of a greeting. "The lake ice is breaking."

"It's a real late run for the steelhead," Doug says. "You're just in time."

"Any minute now, any minute now," Jack says, his mind full of the long, dark bodies of fish in the river, and then, "You've got a reading in forty-five minutes, then a dinner that should be over by ten, the president of the local community college wants to meet you. At midnight, we fish."

By 12:25 A.M. I am dressed in my long underwear, Jack's camouflage sweat clothes, Mike's neoprene liners, Doug's waders and Nick's hat. I look like the Michelin tire man, the waders so big and stiff I can barely put one foot in front of the other. We pile into Mike's Montero, rods and reels jangling in the back. Jack and Mike and Doug and I. Nick, each man has told me (privately, in a quiet, apprehensive voice), is recovering from bursitis and a divorce, and for one or the other of these reasons, he will not fish this year.

No one asks me if I'm tired, nor do I ask them. These men

have had nine months of winter to catch up on their sleep, cabin fever reflecting in their eyes like exclamations. The steelhead will start running soon, maybe tonight, and there is no question about where they should be.

It takes almost an hour to get to the river with what I quickly understand is an obligatory stop at the Sunoco in the tiny town called Honor for day-old doughnuts and Coca-Cola and banter with the cashier. Along the way we listen to what Mike and Jack say is their latest road tape, three Greg Brown songs recorded over and over to fill a ninety-minute drive. "Gonna meet you after midnight," say the lyrics repeatedly, "at the Dream Cafe."

The rotating sign on the Honor State Bank says 1:51 A.M. and twenty-two degrees. The men have bet on what the temperature will be. They have also bet on how many cars we will pass on the two-lane highway, how many deer we will see in the woods between Mike's house and the bridge, if it will snow or rain and, if so, how hard (hardness gauged by comparison with other nights' fishing). Doug wins the temperature bet, closest without going over, at twenty-one degrees.

The betting is all part of a long, conversational rap among them, a rap that moves from Mike's last fish to Jack's latest fiction to concern for Nick and his lost house to the girl at the Sunoco to an in-unison sing-along to their favorite Greg Brown lyrics. The whole conversation is less like speaking, really, and more like singing, a song they've spent years and years of these cold spring nights together learning, nights anybody anywhere else in the world would call winter, nights filled with an expectation that can only be called boyish and shadowed by too much of the grown-up knowledge that can utimately defeat men.

Sometimes they remember I am there, sometimes they forget I am a woman.

I feel, in those moments, like I've gone undercover, like I've been granted security clearance to a rare and private work of art. And though I have always believed that women bond faster, tighter, deeper than men could ever dream of, there is something simple and pure between these men, a connection so thick and dense and timeless that I am fascinated, and jealous, and humbled, all at the same time.

"Shit," Jack says, "Look at 'em all." We have come finally out of the woods and to a bridge no longer than the width of the two-lane roadway. As impossible as it is for me to believe, at two A.M. the gravel areas on both sides of the bridge are lined with pickups, a counterculture of night stalkers, two and three trucks deep.

I can see by the posture of the men who line the bridge and look gloomily over the edge that they do not teach poetry at Interlochen Arts Academy. One of them staggers toward the truck, reeling drunk. A boy of nine or ten, dressed all in camouflage, tries to steady him from behind.

"They ain't here yet," the old man says, an edge in his voice like desperation. "It may be they just aren't coming."

"They'll be here," Jack says, easing himself out of the Montero and steering the man away from the broken piece of bridge railing. "It's been a long winter for everybody," Jack says, almost cooing, and the old man drunkenly, solemnly, nods.

Mike pulls me out of the truck and hands me a flashlight. We creep to the edge of the bridge and peer over. "Just on for a second and off," he whispers. Even to me it is unmistakable; the flashlight illuminates a long, dark shape already half under the pylon. "Don't say anything," Mike mouths to me soundlessly. Jack leaves the old-timer to sleep in his car and joins us. Mike holds up one finger, and Jack nods. "We'll go downstream," Jack says, after some consideration. "Nobody's gonna do any good here."

We drive downriver while Mike points out all the sights as if we can see them—a place called the toilet hole, where Doug and Nick got lucky, the place Mike got his car stuck so bad four-wheel drive couldn't help him, the place Jack caught last year's biggest fish. We can see the headlights of people who are smelt-dipping out where the river empties into the lake, and a red and white channel marker lit up and looming in the darkness, its base still caked with lake ice and snow.

We drop Doug off at his favorite hole near the mouth of the river, drive back upstream a few hundred yards, park the Montero and step out into the night.

"It's a little bit of a walk from here," Mike says, "and the mud's pretty deep." It is impossible for me to imagine how I will move my stiff and padded legs through deep mud, how, at twenty-two degrees, I will step into that swift and icy river, much less stand in it for a couple of hours. I can't imagine how, with all these clothes and pitch dark around me, I'll be able to cast my fly with anything resembling grace.

Two steps away from the truck and already I feel the suction. The mud we are walking in ranges from mid-calf to mid-thigh deep. I'm following Jack like a puppy, trying to walk where he walks, step where he steps. I get warm with the effort, and a little careless, and suddenly there's nothing beneath me and I'm in watery mud up to my waist. Mike and Jack, each on one arm, pull me out of the hole so fast it seems like part of the choreography.

"Let's try to cross the river," says Jack, and before I can even brace for the cold, we are in it, thigh . . . hip . . . waist . . . deep, and I feel the rush of the current tug me toward Lake Michigan. "One foot in front of the other," Jack says. "The hole's right in front of you; when you're ready, go ahead and cast."

I lift the rod uneasily into the night, close my eyes and try to remember how they did it in *A River Runs Through It*, and then bring it down too fast and too hard with an ungraceful splat. "Let out a little more line," Jack says, so gently it's as if he is talking to himself. A few more splats, a little more line, and I am making casts that aren't embarrassing. Jack moves without speaking to help Mike with a snarl in his line. "This is your night, Delp," Jack says, his shadowy form floating away from me, a dark and legless ghost.

What in the world are you doing here? a voice giggles up from inside me, and the answers sweep past me, too fast to catch: because I can't turn down a challenge, because my father wanted a boy, because touching this wildness is the best way I know to undermine sadness, because of the thin shimmery line I am seeing between the dark river and the even darker sky.

Soon I stop thinking about being washed to Lake Michigan. I marvel at how warm I am in the waders, so warm and buoyant that I forget myself from time to time and dip some unprotected part of me, my hand or my elbow, into the icy water. A deer crackles sticks in the forest across the river; an angry beaver slaps his tail. In whispers we take turns identifying planets and constellations—Ursa Major, Draco, Cassiopeia, Mars and Jupiter—and murmur at the infrequent but lovely falling stars.

When we are quiet I can hear a faint crashing—constant, reverberant—sounding in the dark for all the world like the heartbeat of the Earth. "Lake Michigan coming over the break-water," Jack says to my unasked question. "There must be a big wind on the other side."

My fishing is steadily improving: every fifth or seventh cast hangs a long time in the air and falls lightly, almost without sound.

"You know," Jack says, "there aren't too many people who

could come out here like this and not hook themselves or me or the shoreline . . . isn't that right, Delp?" Mike murmurs in agreement, and my head swells with ridiculously disproportionate pride.

The constellations disappear, and a light snow begins falling. "God, I love the weather," Mike says, his voice a mixture of sarcasm and sincerity, and for a while there is only the whisper of the line and the flies.

"Fish!" Jack shouts suddenly. "Fish on the line!" I am startled almost out of my footing, as if I've forgotten what we've come for, as if the silence and the night and the rhythm of the flies hitting the water have become reason enough. We reel in our lines and watch Jack land his fish. It is long and thin, and its speckled belly gleams silver as it thrashes in the tiny beam of the flashlight. Jack looks at us helplessly, delighted by his luck and skill and yet wishing, simultaneously, that it had been me who caught the fish, wishing even harder, I can see, that it had been Mike.

We fish a little longer, but now there's no need to stay. The spell has been broken; the first steelhead has been caught in its journey up the Platte.

"Let's wade downriver a little," Jack says, when we've reeled in our lines, "to try and avoid the mud." I take short rapid breaths as we move through the water. "This part is deep," Jack says. "Take it slow."

The water creeps up my chest and into my armpits; I'm walking, weightless, through a dark and watery dream. For a moment there is nothing but my forward momentum and the lift of water under the soles of my boots that keep me from going under. Then I feel the bank rise suddenly beneath my feet.

"No problem," I say, just before my foot slips and I do go

under, head and all into the icy current. I thrash my arms toward shore, and Jack grabs me. "Better get you home," he says, as the cold I've ignored for hours moves through my body with logarithmic speed. "You've gotta meet students in a couple hours." Back at the truck Doug is curled under a blanket like a dog.

The next day Jack sleeps while Mike makes sure I meet my classes. The students are bright, skeptical, interested. My head buzzes with the heat of the all-nighter, a darkness, like the river dark, threatening to close in. Mike and I drink bad machine coffee in one of the tunnels that connects the English department to the other school buildings, tunnels to keep the students from getting lost in the storms that bring the blowing snow.

"It's hard to explain how much I love these guys," Mike says suddenly, as if I've asked him. "I don't know what I'd do without what we have."

The cement walls of this poor excuse for a lounge move in on us like the weather, and this poet who more resembles a wrestler looks for a moment as if he might cry.

It is late in the evening. I have met three classes, talked to at least thirty students, given another reading, signed books in Traverse City, and as part of an orgy of a potluck, cooked elk steaks, rare, on the grill. Mike, in his other favorite role of DJ, plays one moody song after another on the stereo: John Prine, John Gorka and early Bonnie Raitt. We are all a little high from the good food and tequila. Mike's ten-year-old daughter Jaime and Jack dance cheek to cheek in their socks on the living room floor.

"So are we gonna do it?" Jack says when the song ends, a sparkle in his eyes that says the river is always in him, whether he's standing in it or not. This fish and fiction marathon is in its thirty-eighth hour, and I am beyond tired now to some new level of consciousness.

I have spent too much of my life proving I can be one of the guys, never saying uncle, never admitting I'm tired, or hurting or cold. Tonight I am all three, but the thing that makes me nod my head and say yes I want to go back again and stand in that icy river has nothing, for a change, to do with my father, or my childhood, or all the things in the world that I need to prove. It is the potent and honest feeling between these men that I covet, that I can't miss an opportunity to be close to. I have stumbled, somehow, onto this rare pack of animals who know I am there and have decided, anyway, to let me watch them at their dance. I want to memorize their movements. I want to take these river nights home with me for the times when the darkness is even heavier than it is in this Michigan sky.

A flurry of rubber and neoprene, and we're back inside the Montero. Greg Brown is singing the song about the laughing river. "This is your night, Delp," Jack says, "I can feel it." Around the next bend will be Honor's scattered lights.

JENNIFER SMITH

Cheeseballs and Emergers

I BECAME A fly fisher, not because of aesthetics or passion, or politics or trend, but because when I was growing up we had fly rods in the garage. When we went camping my father always packed the fly rods in the car, handing them to us when we came in sight of water. My older brother and I tossed Royal Wulffs as big as wine corks over the lakes and rivers of our youth never questioning our parents' style of fishing or type of gear. We were fishing and we were content.

During our travels, my brother and I observed other kids' and families' fishing methods—we watched from a distance as cheeseballs were carefully rolled and pressed onto hooks or as worms were pinched from Styrofoam containers and speared into contorted S-shapes. We had seen the big red and white plastic bubbles that went "splat" when they hit the water and floated like buoys. It all looked so strange to us, but we were curious, and when we had the chance, we tried to cast spinning rods and chuck shiny Mepps lures over the water with the strength, grace and skill that our peers did.

Our attempts were fruitless, and I must confess that to this day I can't coordinate the pressing and releasing of the button on a spinning rod. I am hopeless. With all my might I wind up and throw forward, but the line always stops short and slingshots the metal lure back in my face with a jangle, jangle, jangle. Either that, or I let go too soon, and the lure lands behind me in the water.

Although I have heard stories and have witnessed firsthand that food, animals and animal by-products on the end of a hook are effective, I have always stood by the familiar and what has worked for me. I never thought I would feel inclined to exchange my fly rod for a spinning rod. To be honest, my lack of skill influenced this decision more than anything.

But I have been in situations where my imagination wandered and I wondered if my luck would have turned luckier if I had had a spin rod with something shiny and smelly twirling at the end of the line. But as a fly-fishing guide, I have been coached to avoid impure thoughts involving the augmentation or alteration of the natural condition of a reputable fly. "If God had wanted us to fish with worms, they'd grow on the backs of elk or in the necks of chickens," I had been told. But once, just once, I allowed my imagination to go too far. I'm not proud of what I did; in fact, I would like to blame it on an evil twin, but instead,

I will share my story like a person on a talk show who publicly confesses a personal crime. I leave myself open for the audience to wing rotten verbal tomatoes at. I am willing to do this because I discovered something about myself, something I did not realize I needed to know.

My partner in crime was a client whom I had taught and guided for nearly three years. Lynn looks forward to her annual family vacation in Montana with her husband and two children. Her husband likes to fish, too, but he insists on looking after the kids and shoos her off the lodge's front porch so she can take a few days to fish undisturbed by the demands of the family. Over the years Lynn and I have become friends. She lets me critique her casting, I let her critique my divorce. I tell her to stop popping the cast forward, she says to contact her husband's law firm if I need a second opinion. We post photos of each other's children above our computers.

Because I knew she would like the adventure, and because I wanted her to catch some large fish, I had planned a special trip for Lynn that summer. I wanted to show her new and beautiful surroundings and help her catch lots of fish. She has the patience, temperament and appreciation for the sport that makes her a real angler at heart. She loves everything about being in the outdoors and on a river, and so, when the fishing is slow and conditions are tough, she is the one a guide will make silent bargains with God for. "Please, dear God, just one fish. Just give Lynn *one* nice fish. We'll take whatever you can give us, and we'll put it back. Just one fish and I won't wish for anything more. I promise to be satisfied with just one." There are other clients who inspire less, and for those clients who have in some way offended, pressured or ticked-off the guide, the only prayers that go up are for small white fish.

That day we drove for an hour before we reached the trail-head. I was shocked at the number of cars in the parking lot—more than twenty. Surely they wouldn't all belong to fishermen. I rationalized my worries away with the thought that the cars belonged to day hikers or back-country campers. We donned our gear, stuffed the lunches in the backpacks, locked the car and were on our way. The trail was steep, and we took short breaks to rest. At one point we stopped to let a fishing party on horseback pass. The outfitter wore a sweat stained cowboy hat, and a neutral expression. He nodded in recognition of our presence, took a drag on his cigarette, and exhaled. The smoke wafted over his shoulder and sparked memories of Western bars and John Wayne. The riders sat slouched and relaxed, their rods tied securely to their saddles. Each man turned politely to smile and returned to study the space between his horse's ears. Except for a few snorts from the animals, the group passed in silence. Women with fly rods do not have the shock value they once did. Taking out my mental note pad, I wrote down, "Men on horseback look comfortable. Will be fresh by time they get to creek. Will have more time to fish. Women on foot will be tired. Get phone number of outfitter off horse trailer in parking lot."

Lynn and I continued on the hike admiring the colors and quantity of Indian paintbrush, hare bells, and fireweed. A doe and spotted twins let us photograph them before they shied away into the timber. At the top of the ridge we stopped to take in the view of the valley we had just come from. We could see where the trail dropped and would deliver us to our destination on the other side—where large cutthroat trout were rumored to sip and suck and cooperate with anyone who tossed an elk hair caddis, hopper or Royal Wulff in front of them. We happily marched on.

After twenty more minutes, Lynn asked, "How much further?" I had already begun to worry about the same thing, but for other reasons. I was feeling a little guilty since I'd neglected to tell Lynn I had never fished this place before. I had seen enough slide shows and read enough magazine articles to feel like I had been there before but, the truth was, I hadn't. Scary feelings rushed in. The scary feelings intensified when the river finally came into sight, revealing fishermen elbow to elbow along its banks.

Fly fishermen stood staring and casting into the slow quiet waters that wound in oxbow curves throughout the open valley. Fly lines bright and wet were flying in the mid-morning light. It looked like a casting clinic.

The group of horseback-riding fishermen were among the crowd. The outfitter sat in the grass watching over his dudes, puffs of smoke trailing toward the sky. He turned and stared at us, and then the entire creek gazed our way. There is nothing wrong when people notice you making an entrance. In fact, it can be flattering. But fishermen don't like crowds, and I felt like we had walked in on a private conversation, and that we should quietly turn around and go back where we came from. Maybe they only looked up to make sure we weren't bears, but collectively we realized the fishing spot was getting crowded. We needed to spread out, but in order to do so, we would have to walk by and around all the men who were there.

I felt my confidence heading down the trail and I began to question: "Maybe I should hike up another two miles. I remember someone said it was good there. Why are all these people here if it's better up there? Why didn't I fish this before bringing a client? What should I do?" I continued to beat myself up until Lynn interrupted me, "Well, we came to a popular place. There must be some fish here." She was right about that, and I tried to put the possibilities for success back into the day.

Smiling with heads held high, I stepped into the meadow acting as if I did it all the time. Lynn followed me past the fishing in progress. "Hello. Good morning. Hi. Hello. Hi. Good morning." As we offered our greetings, I noticed one important fact. No one was catching anything.

I have pride, but sometimes I am able to abandon my poker face and ask, "How's the fishing?" The man who answered wore a hat that looked like he had sat on it, and a fishing vest appropriately decorated with surgical instruments for clipping, snipping, and extracting. He wore an expression of frustration and sorrow, a man in need of a therapist. With the surgical appliances dangling around his neck and the look of desperation on his face, I would not have been surprised if he had hollered, "*Nurse!*" He shook his head and said, "I fished all day yesterday and since early this morning, and I can't get anything to work. You can see them feeding on something really small. They sit on the bottom and then come up to something tiny. The fish are huge. Look at them. I can't figure it out. I thought if I came early when it was cooler. . . . Maybe we need some cloud cover. Maybe I should try something big. I've tried everything. I've emptied my fly box. It's tough. Just really tough."

As he spoke, a large cutthroat rose quietly to the surface, sipped and sank down. "See!" said the fisherman dropping his shoulders and sounding like a kid whose building blocks had just been knocked over by his older brother, "See that!"

An uncomfortable silence followed. Clearly the man was distressed. We looked at the river and back at our feet. Resigned to his tough luck he said, "You have a good day. I hope you can figure it out. I sure can't."

We trudged past the tenth gentleman in a half-mile stretch.

Cutthroats lined the edges of the creek. Where there was a boulder or a depression, there was a fish. Every riffle was home to at least one native. The sight of these large trout feeding and resting quietly within reach had tweaked my angling instincts. I felt my confidence returning. We could get one to take. I just had a feeling.

I began by tying on a small #18 sparkle dun for Lynn. Minutes later I had her switch to a smaller #20 sparkle dun. After observing the hoppers in the grass, I had her switch to a hopper pattern. Then we changed to a beetle, an ant, a Griffith Gnat, Adams, Parachute Adams, Royal Wulff, Royal Humpy, elk hair caddis, then back to a beetle. I was changing flies like a teenager changes clothes before a big date. The dry-fly patterns failed, so I switched to the wet-fly patterns. We sank pheasant tail nymphs, midge pupae, caddis larvae, all in assorted sizes and colors. In exasperation I tied on a black woolly bugger and had Lynn strip it so close to a fish that it bumped it on the nose. The cutthroat just moved over to let the fly go by. Trout were rising on a whim of their own to an emerging insect we could not see or identify. I began to make bargains with God: "Please dear God, just give Lynn one..."

After two hours of fishing we hadn't gotten a thing. And neither had anyone else on the creek. The sun was high and hot, the wind still. I was feeling tense, and when the buzzing of flies began to sound like lawn mowers, I decided to break for lunch.

We sat on a boulder overlooking a deep pool where several large cutthroats rested. Occasionally, one would shimmy over to a new place on the creek bottom. It was like looking at an aquarium in a doctor's office. Everyone was waiting. Watching and waiting.

We ate our turkey and Swiss sandwiches quietly. I didn't

even have the chocolate chip cookie to look forward to for dessert, since in my nervous haste, I had eaten it earlier that morning.

We continued to study our targets below. Out of boredom and curiosity, I pinched off a piece of bread from my sandwich and flicked it into the pool. As soon as it hit the water I felt a little strange, as if I had thrown a pop can out of my car window. As I reflected on this, a dark shadow rose from the bottom, sipped the bread and dove back down. "Lynn," I said quietly, "did you see that?"

"Do it again," she prodded.

Again the bread crumbs brought the hard-sell cutthroats up to the surface. I quickly looked around to see if anyone was watching. I needed a simple hook that would hold the bread: I grabbed a small midge pattern called a brassie and quickly pressed the bread around it.

The moment ran away with me. I barely stopped to look at Lynn and ask, "Do you think I should do this?"

Lynn nodded, "See if it works," she encouraged. I flopped the breaded hook into the pool. As it hit the water, the bread fell off the hook, and two cutthroats came up and ate the crumbs. I was delighted and bothered at the same time. This was not fly fishing. This was not really fishing at all, but playing with the fish. This was not supposed to be fun, but it *was* fun. "I need something that will stay on the hook," I said out loud. Suddenly, a childhood memory flickered into focus. CHEESE. CHEESE-BALLS.

I opened my sandwich and pulled out the cheese. I carefully pinched off a piece of it, squeezed it onto the hook, and offered it to the trout below.

All eyes were upon us as we netted the eighteen-inch cutthroat. Downstream the sound of someone spooling their reel pierced the silence that followed the excitement we had caused. It was the frustrated fly fisherman we had met earlier, and he was walking toward us.

Lynn and I were like two schoolgirls in a library. The more we tried not to laugh, the funnier everything became. The fisherman watched while we photographed, admired, and released our catch. Standing innocently and quietly beside us he asked, "What'd ya catch it on?"

Taking the opportunity to burn in Hell, I replied, "A Prince Nymph."

Trying to avoid all evidence, I even lied about the fly I had stuck the cheese to. Lynn watched our conversation like someone watching the ball at a tennis match.

"I have a few more if you'd like to try one."

I removed one off my vest and held it out to him with a smile.

"No. No thanks. I've tried one of those already. How did you fish it?"

"Downstream."

"Okay. Well, I'll just have to keep trying. "

After he left, Lynn and I packed up the remains of our lunch and moved a little further downstream to avoid the prying stares from our audience. She caught two more cutthroats on the cheeseball fly, while I checked on the mood of the fishermen along the bank.

Nobody else had caught a fish. Some fishermen were leaving for other parts of the creek.

Oddly enough, after we had had our fun, I felt defeated. It did not feel as if the fish we caught counted. I felt too much like I had cheated myself, like the way a person feels when she has cheated at solitaire. What was the matter with me? It was just fishing; we were laughing and enjoying ourselves—wasn't that the whole point? Did I take myself too seriously? I guess what I know is that I like challenge, and for me, fly fishing is a great puzzle-solving challenge. When I have made a difficult cast and landed it the way I wanted, or fished over a difficult fish and finally caught it, I feel true reward. I didn't feel the same catching a trout with cheese.

We both admitted later that we had had a great time and that we would never forget the looks of disbelief on the men's faces up and down the creek when they saw us catching fish. But that day I learned that, for me, there is something truly satisfying about catching fish on flies. The cheeseballs had kept us entertained, but it just wasn't the same. I became a fly fisher by habit, but on that trip I emerged a true fly fisher. To this day, I am more than willing to take my defeats as I deserve them, and the cheese stays in the sandwich.

MALLORY BURTON

Blood Knots

I HAVE NEGLECTED to tie the wading boots properly, to pull the braided laces tight against the metal grommets, to fasten them securely with a double knot. This is partly due to lack of effort and partly because the boots are much too big for me. They belong to my father. Belonged to my father. I suppose they are mine now. Neither my mother nor my sister fishes. I am the only one.

The boots are full of fine gravel, which chafes between my thick, outer wading socks and the lightweight fabric of these summer waders. I should get out of the river to empty the boots, but it doesn't seem worth the effort of battling the current all the way back to the bank.

A mosquito buzzes close to my temple. I can hear its thin whine over the rushing of the steam, see the dark fluttering blur out of the corner of my eye. The insect lands, and I feel its sting, such a tiny prick that I wonder why I have always made such a fuss about them, slapping at myself and smearing poisonous oil all over my face and limbs.

I slowly raise my hand to my temple and crush the mosquito. Not because I really want to, but because I feel I should. The same way that I felt I should wash my face and comb my hair and put on my clothes this morning, even though it seemed to make such little sense. It is unsettling, this doubting of routine, this absence of concern, this lack of energy. Perhaps I should not be here on the river at all.

"Go. Get out of the house for a while," my mother insisted. She extended her arms and flicked her hands at me as though I were a bothersome child. "There's really nothing you can do until this afternoon."

My father died two days ago. The funeral is today at four. Mother is handling it pretty well. My sister is distraught, sedated. I am still waiting for my own emotion to surface in what I anticipate will be a sense of overwhelming loss. Every few hours, I test the depth of my grief, sounding its progress with tentative excursions into the past.

Earlier this morning, I sorted through my father's fly fishing gear. I have gear of my own, of course, but it isn't something you think of packing when your father has died suddenly and you are trying to catch a plane at an impossible hour. I sorted his flies and mended his leaders. I removed the spool from his old Hardy reel to change it over from a right-handed to a left-handed retrieve. I had to unwind all the line in order to rewind it onto the spool in the opposite direction.

The gear was spread out all over the kitchen floor. A neighbor woman, who'd come by with a tray of baking for after the service, had to pick her way through the mess. Seeing the tangle of line on the floor, she offered to help. She held the line with a slight tension so that I could wind it more evenly onto the spool. She kept looking at the split-cane rod lying in sections near her feet. My father's name had been burned into the shaft in an old-fashioned, flowing script.

"This is beautiful old gear," she said. "Are you going fishing?"

"Yes."

"You're not," said my mother. She shut off the running water and turned, twisting her hands in her apron.

"You said get out of the house."

"I thought maybe a walk." She shrugged and left the room. I expected the neighbor woman to follow her, instead, she motioned me to continue my winding.

"Do you think it's strange, going fishing? At a time like this, I mean?"

The woman hesitated. Then she leaned forward and said, very quietly, "Sometimes it takes a while to catch up with you. When Alex passed away, I didn't even cry. A couple of weeks later I was coming through the door with my arms full of groceries, and the wind caught the door, slammed it shut behind me. I put down the groceries, opened the door and slammed it again. I must have slammed it twenty times."

I pictured the slight gray-haired woman slamming the door, understanding her satisfaction with the final, solid sound of it.

The hatch is beginning. At first there is just a handful of bugs coming off the water, teasing a few eager fish into splashy rises. The nearest fisherman is a hundred yards upstream, stationed in one spot, not casting. Presumably he is waiting for the better fish to show themselves. He looks alert, expectant as the swarm of swallows gathering overhead.

I know this river. The hatch will gradually accelerate over the next hours or so, until the smooth surface of the water is frothed and silver with feeding fish. Until the air is both noisy with lunging rises and soft with clouds of pale-winged mayflies.

The upstream fisherman has his rod in the air now, stripping line with his left hand while the length of his backcast grows. I have picked out my fish as well, a trout that shows the curved half-circle of his back with each leisurely rise. The fish is directly across from me.

I drop a delicate Pale Morning a few feet upstream, floating it dead-drift over his lie. I am in the right place, with just enough slack in my line to ensure a drag-free float, but my timing is off. The bugs are hatching in greater numbers now, and it is difficult to focus on the rhythm of my trout with fish rising sporadically on every side.

One larger fish, in particular, is coming up just a rod length away. His appearance is erratic, and his unexpected rises have twice startled me into lifting the tip of my rod, a reaction that makes the fly take a sudden skip over the water. Afraid that I will spook my fish, I decide to deliberately put down the erratic riser.

I face upstream, waiting for the fish to surface again, quickly stripping in my line until most of it lies in a tangle, bunched against my waist by the current. A cloud passes over the sun momentarily, and the water goes steel-gray. When the fish shows, I slap the line down hard on the water's surface just behind his head. The fish snaps up the natural that was his target, then lunges sideways, seizing my imitation and taking it down with him.

For a few seconds the leader disappears, its surface coils pulled straight down by the fish. Then, with a great sucking splash, the trout suddenly shoots through the air. He is coming fast, straight at me, eye level. His mouth is open, and I can see the fly lodged securely in his upper jaw. His gills are flared open. Looking into his mouth and out through his gills, I can see the trees on the far shore. The fish is wide-eyed, and I wonder if he has seen me. He drops just short of hitting my chest, clumsily on his side, throwing water in my face.

The fish changes direction, runs upstream. The current does not appear to be much of a deterrent. The pile of line at my waist diminishes rapidly, and somehow I have the sense to let it go, to keep my hand off the reel. The last of the slack disappears, and the line slaps tight against the rod, sending out a shower of tiny droplets. For an instant I feel the weight of the fish connecting at the other end of the line in one strong pull, and then he is gone.

Damn. Damn. I want that fish. I lift the rod tip, aching for the fish to be there. I will play the fish carefully and bring him gently to the net. I will hold him in the current, admire his colors until he is strong enough to swim away on his own; instead, the line comes back easily through the water.

The fish will jump again, trying to shake the fly that is still hooked in his jaw. I will see the gleam of silver as his twisting body catches the sunlight. I stand looking upstream, but he does not show.

It is difficult to retrieve the line. My hands are shaking, and I feel weak, disoriented. The current tugs at my legs with a new intensity, as if the river has suddenly risen six inches. In turning, I lose my footing. My feet slide over the smooth stones and gravel bottom of the river, carried by the current. It occurs to me that if I fall, I will not have the strength to regain a footing. I concentrate on remaining upright, leaning into the current, angling slowly across the river toward shallower water and the protection of a small island. Slowly I make my way to the water's edge and sit down heavily on the bank, where I lie back in the rushes, my feet tailing in the water.

My father's death was sudden, unexpected. The secretary found him face down on his desk when she went in with the morning mail. It is difficult to believe. He was the sort of man you'd expect to perish on the side of a mountain heading for the continental divide. Or on the bank of an icy river during the winter steelhead run.

The sun is warm on my face. A mayfly, a survivor, crawls up on the underside of a reed and hangs upside down on its tip, swaying. There is a cold spot on my right instep where the gravel in my father's boot has finally punctured a small hole. It is just as well. If I get off the river now, I will just have time to drive back and change for the funeral.

I sit up and quickly untie the boots, keeping one eye on the river. I dump the gravel, rinse the boots, and retie the laces with a secure double knot. I repair the leader, adding lengths of fresh tippet with a series of secure blood knots. I carefully attach a new fly. The hatch could go on for hours. There are still plenty of fish rising. I wonder if my mother and sister will understand.

ALLISON MOIR

Love the Man, Love the Fly Rod

I FELL IN love with a fly fisherman. Not a unique feat, by any means. Estimates are there are five million fishing widows out there.

My fly fisherman spends winter weekends hunched over his fly-tying vise tying black ants and watching good ol' boys catch catfish on TV, who say things like "Shoooeee, that's a big 'un there, Billy." Come Opening Day, I lose him to dawn hatches and evening rises. My freezer becomes a morgue—trout, neatly wrapped in brown-paper body bags. I complain to friends, "I can't believe my competition is *fish*, and not other women."

Finally, at the end of another weekend left at home—in a

weakened mindset of can't-beat-'em-join-'em—I ask to be taken fishing.

John's eyes light up as if I were the prom queen asking the class geek on a date. "Really? You want to go fishing?" Then, more pessimistically: "Are you sure?"

No, I'm not sure. It is decidedly *not* the prospect of standing in a cold stream for hours waiting to catch a defenseless little trout, *thonk*ing it on the head, gutting it, stuffing it with butter, dill or rosemary, salt and pepper, tossing it onto the grill, then eating it with an "I caught this" satisfaction that has piqued my interest in fishing. But hey, love is blind. Love the man, love the fly rod.

So I vow to give fly fishing one season, from June to September, one season of valiant, unwavering interest. If I don't like fishing by then, then the sport is all his. No nagging—I promise.

As lionesses are better hunters than lions, I'm told (not by my love, it should be mentioned) that women are often better fishermen than men. Rosalyn Carter and Hadley Hemingway beat out Jimmy and Ernest on streams. And, of course, champion distance-caster Joan Wulff, who was married to the late Lee Wulff, runs a fly-fishing school in New York.

According to a fishing guide friend, it's because we women have better hand-eye coordination; we pay more attention; we read the water better, and we also lack that simple American male arrogance. "You weren't born thinking you know how to @*!# and fly fish," he told me. History, too, is on our side: the first person to write about fly fishing was Dame Juliana Berners, the nun and noblewoman who wrote *The Treatyse of Fysshynge wyth an Angle* around 1421.

So maybe my hopes are just a little too high as John and I set out for our first experience fishing together. I am unrecognizable, an Orvis catalog parody: kitted up in leaking, borrowed waders in men's size XL; a vest bulging with flies, leaders, 5X and 6X tippets; spare reels with dry-fly line and wet-fly line and lead weights; a creel; forceps and toenail clippers hanging on cords around my neck; a wooden net dangling down my back; leader straightener; magnifying glass; penknife; baseball hat and sun-glasses.

The instruction is equally hideous, a series of increasingly tight-lipped *don'ts*.

"*Don't* hold your rod like that. You'll break the tip off if you fall in. Reel first," John barked.

"*Don't* cast downstream!"

"*Don't* cast that far back, or you'll get snagged on the grass!"

"*Don't* snap your wrist!"

"*Don't* put your hand there; that's poison ivy!"

What woman hasn't been here before, in that moment of an-guished understanding that she cannot be taught by someone she loves?

"When we put that fly rod in your hand, you're going to do some terrible, disgusting things with it," instructor Mel Kreiger warns our class straight off. Lined up along the bank of the fabled Henry's Fork, the spring creek in southeastern Idaho, are thir-teen students—aged eighteen to fifty—doctors, lawyers, art dealers and newspapermen. I quickly learn that fly fishing is all about casting: the precise movement of the whippy, lightweight rod that propels the fly line in a fluid, gentle S-curve over your shoulder and out onto the stream.

A no-brainer, I think, watching him demonstrate the roll

cast, the simplest maneuver in all of fly fishing. It's simple: hold your rod straight up so the fly line hangs limply behind, then firmly push the rod forward about six inches. The line should fall straight out on the water.

"You've got to push it, like this," Mike, another instructor, says, taking my rod. He guides my arm, trying to stimulate muscle memory. "Good." He turns away, and my fly line piddles into a heap.

"Keep your wrist tight, like this," Kurt, a guide, shows me. "That's it."

"Let go of your death-grip, like this," Bob, another guide, advises.

"Make the rod go *whuuump*, like this," Mel recommends. "Better."

In fact, I'm not getting any better, as Mel's long-distance shouts of "No good!" make that embarrassingly, publicly clear. Mike, Kurt, Bob and Mel—do all fly fishermen have one-syllable names?—attend to other students. Many of them have progressed to full casts, their orange fly lines slicing through the clear June morning. My pathetic fly line swirls and tangles in the pellucid water, like icing artfully dribbled on a coffee cake.

Diane, an Islamic art dealer in her mid-thirties, also gets the revolving-door of help from all four men. Make that five: her eighteen-year-old stepson foolishly offers advice.

"Here, Diane, just stop your arm right about here, like this," he says, his line landing dead-straight.

"I'm *trying*, David!" she hisses.

Things get better when we move away from the water and onto dry land. We spread out on a mown field, casting S-curves and V-curves, searching for the proper groove. My confidence soars as I do good loops. I feel happy; my mind and body are fixated on making one simple, fluid motion. The surroundings are splendid—fields of blooming Queen Anne's lace and dandelions, woodpeckers hard at work on the regal lodgepole pines, moose standing knee-deep in the Henry's Fork staring—and probably laughing—at what the guides call our "butchered casts."

A little after dawn, I stand with Leon, my guide for the morning, at the edge of the Box Canyon of the Henry's Fork. We are a few miles upstream from where yesterday I perfected my casts—on grass. Leon is unwinching his drift boat from its trailer.

"Point of information," he says, watching me step into olive-green, thigh-high rubber waders. "Get new waders."

"Spend *more* money on this sport?" is my retort. "You must be nuts. I haven't even caught a fish yet." Yesterday, I was out-fitted with bottom-of-the-line equipment—a two-hundred-dollar rod, a fifty-dollar reel, and fifty-dollars' worth of flies stored in a plastic Dixie cup.

"Your waders—they're the most dangerous kind," he re-joins brusquely. "Fill up with water and take you down. I'd never wear 'em on a river out here. In fact," this macho high-school football coach turned fishing guide says, pointing downstream to a roiling, angry section of the river, "someone drowned right there. Water filled up his waders, and he got himself stuck under a fallen log. His wife watched the whole thing."

I look at him, terrified and dumbfounded. Terrified I'll be taken down by this *Jaws*-like river. Dumbfounded that already, my first morning on the river, Napoleonic little Leon has tried to set me—a *girl*—on edge. He has succeeded.

I catch one fish this morning; Leon, the paid guide, tells me I caught five. I come off the river feeling scared, cold, angry and ambivalent. It's a setback. Mutinous thoughts fill my mind like so many angry thunderheads: I'll happily stay at home. *He can have fly fishing.*

But I've committed to one season of this sport, and I can't lose face and give up now. So before I head off to join John in Montana to cement my shaky skills and even shakier interest, I find myself killing time in the outlet stores of Jackson, Wyoming. An awful, practical idea creeps up on me: I could be fishing. The Snake River, after all, winds just outside of town.

Will I remember how to tie an improved clinch knot? What flies should I use? What if I fall in and drown? Do I look foolish all duded-up with equipment? What happens if I, God forbid, catch a fish? The cross-examination is relentless. The next thing I know, I'm there.

I look into the plastic Dixie cup that is my fly box and think about all the elements I should consider in choosing the perfect fly: water temperature, what stage of development the bugs are in, what the fish are eating right now. Then I remember what a guide told me: "Ninety percent of what a trout eats is brown and fuzzy and about five-eighths of an inch long."

I, however, choose the prettiest fly in my meager box—a Royal Wulff Parachute. The red, green, black and white fly preens proudly atop the picnic-blanket-sized tributary of the Snake I choose to fish. Five times, to my amazement and glee, fish rise, and nibble. My God, I think, *I can do this.*

The meandering Ruby River—pebbly riffles where smaller fish thrive, sharply cut curves and deep, clear pools where larger fish live—is the perfect stage on which to show off. It's never deeper than I can handle, never threatening to take me down. This is my graduation, I suppose, from this summer of fishing. Fish are jumping like popcorn in a pan, and John is behaving like an over-excited Little League coach.

"Come on, catch him. Just float the fly down right in front of his nose...No! Not there, you'll scare him...Good. Good. Good. Too much arm...Careful of the rod tip..."

"*You* take the goddamn rod!" I spit back.

"No! I am going to watch you *catch that fish*."

On my third cast, my Blue-Winged Olive lands at the head of the deep pool ten feet ahead of the big brown. The current kicks it out of his feeding lane, but I give it some action—a few quick jerks—and it goes back in the drift. My coach behind me inhales loudly and holds his breath as the fly passes over the fish. It takes my fly and runs, heading toward a thicket of dead branches. "Rod tip up! Rod tip up!" he yells, but it's already up.

I reel in the fish gently. John laughs as I coax it, saying, "Come here, sweet, sweet." I wet my hand and pick up the fish, its sunset orange spots glinting in the bright sun. Water purls around me as I bend down to tug the barbless hook from his pink mouth and hold him facing upstream to force oxygen back into his system. Then I set him free, releasing this wonderful, wild creature as old as the Ice Age, back into the cycle of nature.

I look back at my Big Sweetie, who is grinning in a way I had never seen before. "I really love you," he says quietly.

We spend the afternoon in a quiet dance, leapfrogging each other from pool to pool about three-quarters of a mile upstream. He fishes one pool his way, I fish the next, mine. I feel like I've attained the Zen plateau that is the core of the fly-fishing experience. But my serene state, I realize, is due more to the experience of fly fishing as a shared event; as I reel in my fifth fish, he gives me a thumbs-up from a pool upstream.

⌒

I select the handmade Winston fly rod I plan to give John as a wedding present. What better gift to celebrate this sport we now share? What better symbol of our lives together as a couple of fishers? He tells me, though, that he's not ready for married life.

I hold his hands—those same calloused hands that nimbly tie tiny midges to thin tippet—for the last time, and then let go, gasping for many months like a trout out of water.

I return to the sports I was raised on—hiking, skiing, tennis, golf—and revel in my ability to climb a mountain, do a bump run, a backhand volley, a chip shot.

One mid-summer morning, though, I wake before dawn and drive through thick ground-fog to a small Vermont river John and I had scouted. I haul out my fly rod, my reel, my life-threatening waders, and make my way down the steep embank-ment. The grass tears morning dew as I brush through.

Carefully, quietly, I crunch on the rocks along the still water's edge. At a fast-moving riffle, I wade to the middle of the stream. The pale, lemony light tries to cut the thick fog, and I squint through it, upstream. Recalling lessons from the men who have taught me—John, Mel, Mike, Leon—I fish my way up to a big pool.

The Royal Coachman Parachute floats enticingly on the clear, brownish water; the fly swirls perfectly, convincingly, drag-lessly in the current. I make a cast, then take a step up-stream. One cast, one step, all the way to the head of the pool. Nothing happens. Not a strike. Not a nibble. Not even a look at my fly.

Boredom hovers. I hauled my carcass out of bed for this? I think. This is fun?

Then the fly dips underwater, into the mouth of a small fish. It resists a bit, but soon swims toward me at the same pace I reel in. Kneeling in the water, I scoop the rainbow into my hand. Pink and vulnerable, it is like a newborn baby.

A quietness washes over me as I sit on a large, flat rock that is warming in the sun. That was not a struggle, not a fight, not an act of aggression or conquest, my catching this fish. It was an incredible temporary connection to another animal—amazing wordless moments for me of awe and beauty, of the primality of nature. I feel, as I always do, honored that this beautiful beast sipped my fly.

If John had been on the river this morning, he would have shared a trick learned from a lifetime of fly fishing, and my fish would undoubtedly have been bigger. But he isn't here; he isn't anywhere in my life, and the giddy joy of the rainbow in my hand is tempered by the loss of him.

I pull from the front pocket of my khakis the crushed, plastic Dixie. The next fish, I am mellowly determined, will be larger. I finger the flies in the half-empty cup. They are mostly dry flies, a few are wet. Many are brown, fuzzy and five-eighths of an inch long. There are western patterns and eastern patterns, showy streamers and gold-beaded attractors—a jumble that any scientific fly fisher, die-hard or purist would sniff at. It is, however, a jumble I understand, flies with which I know where and when and how to fish.

I'm thinking like a fly fisher, I realize. For the last few months I had fallen back on an old way of life, but deep in the rivers of my mind, where my truest self resides, I understand now I am a fisher. There, I am knee-deep and alone in a pebbly riffle, standing strong against the current. Competent in casting around a large rock in midstream—not there to please a man—in my mind I have found focus, quiet and happiness in my stream-side solitude.

One, two, three, four times the loose end of the tippet winds around, securing a new fly. Is this the perfect fly for the water temperature, the insect activity, the time of year? Answer: yes. This morning, in the brightening Vermont sunlight, I am making fly fishing mine.

ELIZABETH STORER

Fishing Lessons

LUCY DREW the leader straight out between her fists, stretching it near its limit against the pale morning horizon. Out there, below the sagebrush hills, a cloud of dust hurled along the county road that crossed the flat fields of the valley and twisted up to where she waited. That'll be them, she thought. Right on time.

Two months had passed since Rick and Judy Holbrook had cancelled their usual August reservations for the lodge, begging off for work reasons. The lawyer business must be booming, Lucy had thought, if they couldn't see their way clear to escape the heat of Houston, even for a week. They were friends, really, and she'd been looking forward to guiding them. Disappointed, she had figured she'd have to wait to catch up with them next year. Yet, two days ago the phone had rung and there was Rick's slow Texas drawl on the other end asking her to guide him for a day. He'd be flying up in a corporate jet, he'd told her, and he was bringing along a fellow who wanted to learn to fly fish more than anything. A client, he'd called him.

Lucy spoke through clenched teeth as she held a fly in her mouth and tied on a piece of tippet: a client in *the orl bidness*—no doubt. The energy bust of the late eighties had done little to dampen the enthusiasm of oil company CEOs for fly fishing expeditions to southern Wyoming, she thought. She attached the fly to the hook keeper, wound the line back onto the reel and placed the rod in the holder along the ceiling of her rig.

Gazing across the wide valley, she reasoned that Rick couldn't have asked for a better day. To her way of thinking, the entire year was designed solely to summon September into existence: cool, crisp mornings turning to warm afternoons under a saturated blue sky. Gone were the heat and dust of summer, the hazy, refracted light washed clean in the thunderstorms of August. Now the valley stood bright and clear, its evergreen mountains painted yellow and orange along their folds where aspens spilled onto pale green hills of sage. Down in the bottom land, mule deer and angus mingled, grazing on fields of cut hay. Cottonwood leaves along the river shimmered gold in the breeze, and beneath them, fat, hungry fish moved through the water.

Lucy looked across the valley and pictured how it would look in a few months, slumbering under its mantle of snow, still as the lake basin it once had been. It didn't take much effort to imagine a day when the wind blew fifty miles per hour, the sky dropped sixteen inches of snow and the temperature hovered around ten below. There would be plenty of those days, she knew, but she didn't mind when they culminated in a day like to-day she could remember in February. Nevertheless, she wasn't ready to resign herself to winter, not yet, even when she knew the cold could be as close as tomorrow's dawn. These days were precious and she wasn't going to waste one of them.

It was a perfect day to fish a perfect place, and if ever there was a perfect ranch on which to fish, the Flying C was it. Three miles of blue-ribbon water floated through it, part hay meadows, part canyon; and near where the sediments met the ancient rock, Castle Creek flowed into the river and formed the deepest pool on the upper stretch of the river. The lower half offered exceptional riffle-pool water and was deep enough to hold good fish, even this late in the season. Pocket water broke up long slicks in the canyon, and Castle Creek attracted significant rainbows and browns in spawning seasons. She'd fished it years ago and been impressed, so when Jake Caswell of the Flying C purchased an old freezer from her, she asked him if he wouldn't mind paying her with fishing privileges. It said a lot about her that he'd been willing to oblige.

Ordinarily, Lucy didn't bring clients here, but the guiding season was coming to a close and she'd only had time to fish it once herself. She'd been debating where to take them since Rick had booked her, and she'd decided coming here would be ideal. Great scenery, easy access and waters that had hardly seen a fisherman all season would make it an exceptional day, she hoped.

She heard the old jeep's gears straining up the rise as Rick navigated the rental to where her rig was parked. Rick got out and with a gentle hello gave her a hug. "Come meet Henry," he said and ushered her over to the passenger side of the jeep, where a man in his mid-fifties in a large Stetson stared out the window at them. Rick made the introductions.

"Welcome to Wyoming," Lucy offered.

"I've been here before," Henry Hamilton drawled with the unmistakable roughness of a west Texas accent.

"Is that right?" Lucy asked.

"We had us some oil fields out north of Casper—near Midwest. You know where that is?" he asked rhetorically. "Most godforsaken spot I ever saw in my life. Makes this place look like a goddamned oasis."

Then he spit. It landed about seven inches from Lucy's boot.

Lucy watched Henry's spittle dry slowly in the morning sun as she absently dug the heel of her boot into the dirt. "Mmmm," she volunteered.

Finally, Rick spoke up. "Damn nice down on the river, I'll bet." Lucy looked at him for an indication of annoyance with Henry's behavior, but nothing escaped his cheerful veneer.

"We'll take just one rig down," she said to them. "Let's get your gear loaded into mine."

"Get my stuff, Rick. I've got one more phone call to make." Henry reached down, picked up the cellular phone and began dialing as Rick dutifully opened the tailgate. They loaded the gear into the back of her four-wheel-drive rig, and Henry finally emerged from the passenger side of the jeep. She'd judged him for a big man but was unprepared when he unfolded to a full six feet four inches, nearly a foot taller than she. He carried an extra fifty pounds around his middle that added to his mass. Big men usually didn't intimidate her, but something about Henry Hamilton gave her pause; the bright promise of the day she had felt earlier grew dim in his long shadow.

Turning away from the rig, Lucy let out a piercing whistle that rang out over the hills. Moments later, two dogs bounded out of the brush and leapt into the back of the rig. She shut the hatch and climbed in behind the wheel. Dropping it into four-wheel drive, she turned onto the two-track that branched off the county road and pitched down off the rise toward the river upstream.

Squeezed in with the fishing gear, the two dogs hung their panting heads over the backseat, framing Henry on either side. "The black one's mine, goes by Egis," Lucy called back to him. "A fellow gave him to me a couple of years ago. I'm taking care of the lab for a friend. Frank, he calls him. Short for Franklin."

Henry eyed the yellow labrador retriever. "As in Benjamin?" Rick asked.

"No. Roosevelt."

"No wonder you're such a miserable mutt," Henry said, as he tried to nudge Frank's head away from him. Glancing in the rearview mirror, Lucy saw the dog drooling dangerously close to Henry's suede-patched shoulder.

The rig dropped down into a hayfield and bounced along until Lucy parked it under the shade of an overhanging cottonwood by the river. They got out and began gearing up, and the sound of the water passing over the rocks and the smell of the fresh cut hay lightened Lucy's mood. The dogs took a long drink from the river and sniffed along the bank. Henry wandered off to relieve himself before putting on his waders, and she turned to Rick.

"He's a bit coarse," she said.

"Henry's a hard case, all right," Rick told her. "You should see him in the boardroom."

"He won't listen," Lucy admonished.

"You can make him."

"Hah—he's not one to take orders."

"If anyone can persuade him, you can," Rick told her with a grin.

"Don't flatter me."

"Besides," Rick turned to her, "he's got a soft spot."

"Where?" she demanded.

"Hard to say. Let me know when you find it."

"You just want me to do your dirty work."

"We all have to sing for our supper once in a while, Lucy." Rick nodded in Henry's direction. "Help me out here, won't you?" Henry emerged from the trees and headed back to them.

"All right then," she told Rick with a forced grin. "I'll be the perfect guide."

Rick grinned back, and she remembered that one of the things she liked about him was his intelligent soft-brown eyes edged with humor. A few years back, she'd rowed him and his wife down the river, and she'd learned a lot about both of them in those six hours. Judy was a great woman and a terrific sport, and Rick proved he knew how to listen, even to his wife. Lucy liked that, and she liked that he hadn't expected to be a great fisherman in a day. He understood that, like a good marriage, fly fishing looked easy from the outside. He was the kind of fellow she might have ended up with if her life had taken a different course, if she hadn't come West. But these days she was looking for someone who could better fit the landscape she lived in, someone as open and expansive as the prairie.

Henry removed his hat and carefully placed it top down while he suited up. Lucy noticed the 30X label on the inside band that declared it was made from the highest grade of felt and thoroughly inappropriate as a fishing hat. "Nice hat," she tried.

"Well, shoot, little lady, it better be for what I paid for it." He picked it up and thrust it on his head and looked at her. "You ready?"

Lucy gave Rick instructions to fish the water nearest them, working a dry first—a Blue-Winged Olive or an Adams—and then trying a nymph if the dries didn't produce. Henry and she would go up above, and he could meet up with them for lunch, after which they would all head into the canyon. She took their lunches and six beers, put them in her pack and set off up the field.

Henry kept at her side for the first hundred yards, his strides almost double the length of her own. They climbed a small rise, and he began to breathe harder and fell back. And then he tripped.

"Damn waders. Don't fit worth a damn." Lucy gave him a moment to catch his breath, then led the way down to the river.

At the edge of a quiet pool of slow-moving water where there was plenty of room for backcasts, she took him through the basics: how the rod and line worked together to place the fly at the desired location, roll casts, backcasts, false casts, direction change and line control. She began to relax, comfortable in her role as teacher. Henry's technique was undisciplined at best, nor did he demonstrate much patience.

"I get it," he claimed. "Now, let's find some fish." He held his line in large loops draping down the front of his waders and into the water.

"Okay. But let's put a fly on your line. You'll want to throw more than a leader at them."

"Huh?" He pulled at his line, first one piece, then another until he found the end. The tippet made a slight curve at its end. "No wonder I didn't catch any."

"It broke off on the rocks behind us about twenty or thirty casts ago. Remember, keep your casts in a sloping plane—up behind you, down toward the water in front." She waved her hand at an angle to the horizon. "And get in the habit of putting your line on your reel when you want to change locations. It'll save you time in the long run."

She tied on a small emerger pattern and let him try a few

more casts. When she was satisfied he could land the fly in the water and pick it up again without beating a lather, she moved him up a few yards to the tail of a riffle and had him cast across it and let the fly swing down through the current. Small trout were splashing along the seam between the moving and slack water. She stepped back a few yards, squatted down and watched quietly.

The line caught on itself as a breeze moved down the river. She let Henry untangle it himself. Downstream, she looked for Rick's line flashing in the sun, but saw only the river in motion.

Henry hooked into a small rainbow on his second strike. "Rod tip up," Lucy called to him as she waded over to his side. "Keep a tight line and bring him over into the slow water. Come here, little fellow." She swooped her left hand underneath the fish and gently picked it up by its jaw with her right. The eleven-inch rainbow danced in her hand as she showed Henry how to push the hook back through the side of its lip to release it. "If it's down deep, you're better off to cut the line and let him have the fly." She held the fish for a moment and then slipped it back into the water and let it go.

"That's it?" he asked.

"That's a start," Lucy told him.

He took a long drag on the cigarette he'd lit while she'd unhooked the fish. "Shit. That's no big deal."

He had his fly back in the current and was intently watching it as his cigarette dangled from his lips.

"Every few casts, take a step downstream to cover different water." He did nothing to acknowledge this last instruction and continued to cast, and for a moment Lucy thought he hadn't heard her. Then he abruptly stepped away from her and downstream. Suddenly, she felt her role diminished, reduced from teacher to servant. She knew to expect this from her students to some degree; like raising children, the point was for them to get along without you. Henry would like to think that he grew up on his own, she thought.

"I'm going to take a look at the water above. Yell if you need me." He grunted his acknowledgment as she moved away. Egis happily accompanied her upstream, and Frank bounded out of the willows a few moments later. She tossed him a stick to chase back into the grass and turned to look back at Henry. He stood with his head down, untangling his line. She watched until he began casting again and moved on. Everyone deserved to make their own mistakes without someone looking over their shoulder, she reasoned.

She walked across the smooth, round river rocks and tried to recover the sense of harmony she'd felt before Henry's arrival. His egoism upset the balance of this place, she thought. If you spent any time at all framed by the terrain, a sense of your own small stature was inevitable. She supposed it might be different in a city where all those mirrored facades reminded you of your own self-importance. Here, your only reflection was in the river, and the river was alive and unforgiving. Without distinction, it could echo each impatient expression, fell any careless step. Catching every counterfeit gesture in its current, it could race down the valley, reducing even the largest self-image to the size of a pebble.

By lunch time, Henry had caught six fish, all under twelve inches. Lucy saw Rick come striding up the bank toward them as she opened her pack.

"How'd you make out?" Henry demanded as Rick arrived at the lunch site.

Rick glanced at Lucy for an indication of what success the

morning had brought Henry before answering. She waggled her hand before reaching into her pack. "Beer, anybody?" she asked.

"Sure," Rick said. She handed him a can that he opened and drank from before turning to Henry. "I did all right. A couple of nice ones around sixteen."

"Sound like monsters compared to the bunch of sardines I pulled in," he laughed. "You hear that, missy? Rick's been catching himself some whoppers. You show me where those big ones live this afternoon."

"Have a sandwich, Henry." She tossed him a roast beef and Swiss. She passed another to Rick with a wink. Everyone's mood had brightened since they'd caught fish and Henry's feigned boredom failed to conceal his enthusiasm. She sat down at the foot of a bent cottonwood and drank a beer and ate her sandwich. She listened to a woodpecker knocking away at a tree above and watched the shadows move down the rocks at the foot of the canyon.

"Canyon time's a little different," she said. "Sun's off the water earlier, should be to our advantage." Rick nodded; Henry was off to one side searching through his vest for something. Lucy looked past the river to the hills beyond, a dust of snow still visible on their tops from a storm two days before.

"Hey!" Henry yelled. Lucy and Rick turned to see Henry scowling at Frank. "That blasted hound ate my lunch," he announced. "I put it down right there." He pointed to the ground where only a piece of plastic wrap waved at them from the dirt. Rick and Lucy glanced at each other.

"I've got more," Lucy told him and stood up.

Frank lay down at a short distance and looked up at the three of them with eager brown eyes.

Lucy offered Henry another sandwich. "Keep it," he told

her. "I got all I want right here." He tapped the side of a silver flask, unscrewed its top and took a long pull. "Man's best friend," he muttered and lit a cigarette. He turned to Lucy and said, "I hate people who have dogs. They haven't got the guts to bite people themselves."

After lunch, Lucy sent Rick upstream into the canyon ahead of her and Henry. "Fish below the mouth of the creek," she told him. She and Henry followed on less even footing. A quarter of a mile upriver, she spotted rising fish in a long slick broken by boulders where the shadows widened along the far bank. Henry stumbled behind her, and she smelled the whiskey on his heavy breath. Eyeing the deeper water that lay between the fish and them, she considered whether they could negotiate the currents. It was too good to pass up, she decided, and dropped down to the edge of the water.

"Take my hand," she told him and led him into the water. In no time it rose to just below the top of her waders. She hoped that Henry wouldn't fall because she knew they would both go under, and she'd forgotten to ask him if he knew how to swim. His height kept the water nearer to his middle, and he seemed to bob along with the current. She inched forward on tiptoe, holding tightly to his hand. Then she felt the gravel rise up in front of them, and in another step, the water dropped to her waist and they were out of danger.

Positioning him well downstream of three rising fish, Lucy tied on a size 16 Adams Parachute and demonstrated how to make an upstream cast, watch the fly for a good float and take up the slack. She plucked the fly off the water before a trout could consider it. "Your turn," she said and took a few steps forward and handed Henry the rod.

His first few casts were sloppy and put the fish down, so they moved upstream to some other risers. With a slightly improved cast, he put the fly in all the wrong places, where it got swept underwater. The fish stopped rising there, too. They moved up a little farther to where he finally had a strike and missed it. She knew this wasn't the easiest thing to learn in a day, but she was mad at him for drinking the whiskey at lunch and for thinking he could learn to fish without her.

"There!" she declared when a second fish rose to his fly. He lifted the rod but was too late to set the hook. "When's the last time you got your eyes checked?" she asked.

"I can see the goddamn fly," Henry said and cast again. Two casts later another trout rose, and he yanked so hard on the strike that he broke off the fly. Lucy picked another fly from her hat, reached for his line and tied the new fly on.

"These aren't bass," she said flatly while she greased it up and handed it to him. He whipped the fly back and forth and splattered it onto the water. The fish went down.

"Look," she said curtly. "I want you to try casting about a foot above the river, to help the fly extend out before settling onto the water. It'll help your presentation." Lucy could hear the insolence and impatience in her voice, but she failed to swallow them.

"What are you talking about?" He was like a child who refused to mind. "The fish are in the water, not over it," he scoffed.

"I'm very aware of that, Henry." Later, she would regret the sarcasm. "Give me the rod," she quietly demanded and executed a perfect cast. The fly floated gently down to the water and a trout rose to claim it, but she pulled it away before the fish could hook itself.

"Shit, you missed him," he drawled. "What'd I expect, trying to learn something like this from a girl."

Lucy didn't think she'd heard him correctly. She turned and saw him smiling down at her. Nodding toward the shore behind her, he said, "Rather than messing with this darn thing, I reckon you and me would be better off spending our time lying over there under that tree."

Lucy stared at him for a moment. "I see your vulgar Texan instincts have won out over your southern gentlemanly manners," she said. "If you have any manners at all," she added and, handing him the rod, turned and waded back to shore. Floating on her anger, she crossed the deep stretch in a matter of seconds.

Egis greeted her at the edge of the water, and she reached out to him with a shaking hand. Her face felt flushed, like she had been slapped, and she eased herself down onto one knee and gulped for air. A faint wave of nausea rose up inside her. Goddamn, she thought, I don't need this.

She petted the dog until she felt the queasiness pass, and then she stepped over to where she had left her rod leaning up against a tree and walked upstream a hundred yards. She unhooked her fly and tied on a perfect size 18 Royal Wulff and waded into the water. She worked out some line, cast to a rising fish and hooked it. It was a nice, fat fifteen-inch rainbow, and she played it for a few minutes, brought it in and let it go. Greasing her fly, she took two steps upstream and cast again. She hooked another one and played it well, and she never once looked back at Henry.

By the time Lucy caught her fourth trout, she had moved up into heavier water. She guided the big brown into her net and, laying it on its side in the surface of the water, felt its black eye upon her. Staring back into its eye, she realized she had caught four fine fish and hardly noticed any of them. It was the best fishing she'd had all season, and she wasn't enjoying any of it.

Caught in her own net of anger, she was missing the point. Hell, she thought, I'm the idiot—the bastard meant to make me angry, and he succeeded.

Lucy took a long, deep breath and studied the fish in her hands. It was a perfect fall brown, deep in color and girth, fine-spotted and bright in the afternoon light. For the first time, she held a fish in her hands and knew how it must feel—panicky and confused, frightened and gasping for breath. She unhooked the fly and slipped the fish under the surface of the water and held it there. In and out its cheeks moved at a rapid rate, and she held it until its breathing slowed to her own breath's level pace. Its muscles tightened and its tail trembled, and she felt the wildness in its nature that she could no longer contain. She opened her hand, and it swam away into the deep water of her soul.

She didn't see Rick when he came walking down the bank about the time she landed her sixth fish. Nor did she hear him holler over the tumbling water at her feet. She was completely intent on the river and the fish and was nothing but an extension of the fly and the line and the rod. She was no longer thinking of Henry; he didn't concern her at all. She did, however, hear Frank's one lone yelp that came from behind her, and she turned to see the dog standing erect at the edge of the river. He was looking out at Henry who had tried to make the crossing back to shore, had stumbled and fallen and was now trying to regain his footing while being swept downstream. Lucy watched as he floundered, and then she felt a prickling at her neck. She tilted up her head and held down the back of her hat as the water around her shimmered. The leaves swept down onto the river below her, and she watched as Henry's 30X Stetson shot off his bowed head and landed in the current thirty feet below him—he'd reached for it but was too late. He found a foothold, pulled himself up out of the flood and stood on shaking knees, breathing hard and dripping. Rick hurried down to where Henry was and stood by his side while he caught his breath, and then helped him to shore.

Below, Frank was in the water swimming hard downstream. He covered half the width of the river and then turned back to shore. A minute later, he lumbered up to Henry with the Stetson held gently in his mouth. Lying down at Henry's feet, Frank deposited the hat and wagged his tail.

"You mangy old mutt," uttered Henry. "Why'd you go and do that?" He leaned over to pick up the hat and water sloshed out of his waders onto Frank's nose. Henry turned to Rick. "They say you can lead a horse to water, but you can't make him float."

Henry looked upstream to where Lucy stood. She watched with surprise as he lifted his hat to his head and then, like a gentleman, tipped it in her direction before placing it on his head. Cold water dribbled across his face and down the back of his neck, but he did not wipe it away.

Lucy heard a rise above her and turned upstream to see where it had come from. It had a heaviness and depth to it that spoke of a big fish, so she waited for a full five minutes for it to show itself again and then she caught her breath. She didn't move again for a long time.

Rick and Henry noticed Lucy crouched and still in the midst of gushing water, so they walked up the bank to where she was and watched. She made two casts and then stopped and watched some more. They didn't think she was aware of their presence until they saw the big fish roll about twenty-five feet in front of her and she turned back and looked at them and grinned.

Lucy heard the trout roll again as she watched the two men. Rick motioned with enthusiasm for her to go after it. She turned back toward the fish and watched the water a while longer, and then she wound up her line and waded back to where they were standing.

"How big?" Rick asked.

"Four pounds, maybe five."

"Go get him." Henry said.

"Can't hook him from there," she told them. "There's a snag below his lie that sticks up just far enough to catch your line. You'd have a helluva time setting the hook. The rock's on his left, and there's fast water on his right. He won't go that far. I've tried. The only approach is from upstream."

"Go to it," Rick said.

She looked at Rick and then turned her gaze to Henry.

"You're an ass," she told him.

"So my wife tells me," Henry responded.

"You pissed me off."

"You were very rude," he countered.

"You could learn to have some manners."

"You could learn to lighten up."

Rick broke in. "It just dawned on me."

"What?" Lucy snapped at him.

"The first day I worked for Henry reminded me of something I'd done before. I couldn't place it until now, but it was the first day you took me fishing."

"Not funny, Rick," she told him. She glanced back at Henry, standing soaked to his skin, and then she broke into laughter. "Not true," she giggled, "we aren't alike in the least little bit; I mean, he's all wet."

The men laughed with her, and behind Lucy, the big fish rose again. She looked up at Henry. "Your fish, Henry. You're going to catch that fish," she told him. "And I'm going to show you how."

Henry wavered visibly. "I don't know," he countered. "I'm not sure I'm up to it. Why don't you give it a shot, Rick?"

Lucy didn't give Rick a chance to reply. "The way I see it," she told Henry, "you've got to give it a shot. Or tomorrow you'll get on that jet plane of yours, take off, look down and see the river, and all you'll be able to think about is that you blew a chance to catch a really fine fish. And you can hang up your rod right then and there, because if you were ever to set your big toe anywhere near a trout stream again with rod in hand, the fish would race half a mile in either direction to get away from you. It'd be hopeless. They'd sense your lack of pride and flee."

The two men stared at her in astonishment. She couldn't tell whether they thought she'd just told the biggest whopper of them all or proclaimed to them some divine truth of fly fishing.

"Hogwash," Henry said finally.

"No, no," Rick said. "I've never known her to be wrong about these things."

Lucy wasn't so sure herself, but she waited Henry out. She knew he didn't want to fish anymore, but she was going to make him fish if she could. She stared at the spot where Henry stood and finally, Henry picked up his rod.

"I guess sweat never drowned anyone," he said. "Let's have it."

Henry listened respectfully to Lucy's instructions and gave his full attention to the task. She showed him how to make a downstream drift without too much slack in the line, how to line it up and how to wait a moment longer for the strike to let the fish turn. She critiqued his every cast until she thought he had it right, and then they waded up to the water above the big brown. The sun had been off the river for a half hour, and the temperature was plummeting, but he never complained once, even though his hands were trembling from the cold.

He laid the cast out and flipped the rod tip to let the line out, and the fly drifted down to the fish. When the trout rose up and took it, Henry set the hook, and Lucy felt blessed. For the next fifteen minutes the world shrank to a fish and a hook and a line and a reel and a man with a purpose. He played the fish well, explicitly following Lucy's shouted instructions. She waded up and down the stream and whooped and hollered and generally enjoyed herself. Rick grinned from the bank, drank a beer and watched this curious alliance of man, woman and fish work its magic. Finally, the trout tired and Lucy directed Henry to move it into slow water. As she reached down to net it, the leader broke and just as quickly the fish disappeared under the darkening water. Lucy stood stunned.

"What'd I do wrong?" Henry asked.

It took a moment for Lucy to answer. "Nothing," she said quietly. She reached down into the water and pulled out the fishing line, which ended in a small curl. "It was my mistake; I should have put on a stronger tippet. I completely forgot about it."

"It could happen to anybody, Lucy," Rick offered.

"I can't believe it," she mumbled.

"It doesn't matter," Henry said. "Really. Some pictures would have been nice just 'cause nobody'll believe me without them. But, hey," he shrugged.

"This way the fish can grow every time you tell the story, Henry," Rick told him. "It'll be five feet long by the time we get back to Houston."

"That's true," Henry agreed.

"I'll back you up all the way," Rick told him.

"Is that right?" Henry asked.

"A testifying witness. The whole truth and nothing but."

"I wouldn't mind if you left out a few of the details," Henry appealed.

"I'm a man of the law, Henry."

"Then you know how to use it to your advantage."

"That's right," Rick agreed with a smile.

"You're my kind of lawyer," Henry said as he reached out his hand to Rick. Lucy watched as they shook hands and laughed. They'd already forgotten about losing the fish.

On the way back, Lucy picked up two fish she had caught and cleaned and left on a stringer before lunch. The warmth of the day still radiated from the hayfields as the sun dropped behind the cottonwoods on the far side of the river. At the vehicle she set aside her rod and the fish and began to gather up driftwood for a fire. "Get out of those waders, and we'll have you warm in no time," she called to Henry as she picked up a load of wood. There was a ring of rocks by the river's edge where she stacked the wood and began to break up the twigs and set them up against one another.

Rick was at her side. "I don't think we can stay for dinner," he told her.

"Is Henry that cold?" she asked. "There's a wool blanket in the back of the rig he can wrap up in."

"It's not that," Rick told her. "But Henry says he promised his wife he'd be back by seven. Says she'll worry if he doesn't show up."

Lucy sat back on her heels and looked at Rick. She thought about how she had gotten up at five-thirty that morning to make black bean salad and biscuits. She thought about the two trout she had killed to feed these men. She thought about the bottle of single malt scotch she had been looking forward to drinking while she studied the campfire and watched the sun go down. She thought about how the day began and how it had turned out and she was surprised to discover she wasn't ready to end it quite yet.

She didn't know what to think.

She quit building the fire and drove them to the jeep. The valley stretched below them in the golden light of evening. Rick caught Lucy's arm before she got out. "Here." He held a one-hundred-dollar bill toward her.

She was confused. "The lodge will bill you, like always," she told him.

"Consider it a well-earned tip from both of us."

"Oh."

"Until today, I didn't think I could actually work for the s.o.b.," he told her.

"Until today, I thought you were my friend," she said, and Rick looked wounded. "I'm only kidding, but you've got your work cut out for you," Lucy told him.

"I think we'll do okay," Rick mused. "Thanks."

"I've met worse," she told him. "Good luck."

Henry finished loading the jeep. "That was one helluva fish," he said.

"Helluva fish," said Rick.

"As long as my arm," said Henry.

"Longer," Rick grinned.

Henry turned to get in the jeep, then paused to look off to the north, beyond where the river ran past foothills and hay-fields, past desert and basin, to a place of ancient waters where oil rigs once drew dark riches from the rock but now stood motion-less, creaking in the interminable wind. He turned to Lucy and tipped his hat. "Ma'am," he said and stepped into the jeep.

She watched the men drive away. Down along the river, the

perfect beauty of the barren, black cottonwoods stood silhouetted against the deepening western sky. She thought about the instant Henry had hooked the big fish and she realized she hadn't seen the fish take the fly, because just as Henry had lifted the rod to the strike, she'd looked up to see his face. Henry's eyes had told her that he had hooked the fish and hooked it well, and at the moment when he knew he'd snared it, he'd looked up at Lucy and smiled. Before that, she'd thought of Henry as someone she'd prefer to forget, but now she knew she would never forget his face. She would always remember that instant, and she knew Henry would remember it, too.

The beauty of that moment caught in her throat because she knew so much of life was not like that. So much of life fell short of those perfect, unpredictable moments when you temporarily triumph in the struggle to overcome life's lonesomeness. Fishing, like nothing else, had always provided a line that connected her, not only to fish and rivers and valleys, but to history and family as well; it had grounded her in place and time. As comfortable as she was with its methods, she could never foresee its outcome, and her wonder persisted. Not knowing the effects of the ripples shouldn't stop you from casting out, she reasoned, but sometimes they surprised you. She hadn't expected to be touched by Henry.

Lucy remembered then what the river had taught her, that sometimes fishing was not about fishing at all and that the most memorable trout were never hooked but only imagined in the stillness of a moment sitting patiently on a bank and silently observing her own breath. The self-awareness borne from those moments had helped her to remember who she was, and had helped her to resist the sense of isolation that much of life bestowed. As fleeting as such moments often were, they were what sustained her on days when she felt she had nothing left to give, they were reminders of better times.

She loaded up the dogs and headed down to Jake and Emily's house where she shared the fish and the bean salad and the biscuits. She drank a little more scotch than she'd intended to and stayed a little later than she'd planned. And then she went home.

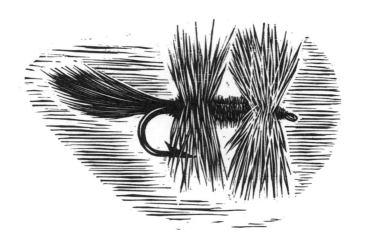

JOAN SALVATO WULFF

A Fly Fishing Life

AS TRUE OF many of the women of my generation who fly fish, my father was a fly fisherman. Mother was not. It became apparent the first time I accompanied them for an evening of fly fishing for bass that Dad had all the fun while Mom got yelled at for not keeping the rowboat at the right distance from bass cover. Unencumbered by the knowledge that women didn't fish, it was obvious to me then, at age five or six, that it was better to be the fisherman than the rower.

My dad, Jimmy Salvato, gave up an accounting job in his mid-twenties to become the proprietor of the Paterson Rod and

Gun Store. Despite a seventy-hour work week, he wrote an out-door column for the *Paterson Morning Call*, helped to start most of the conservation clubs in northern New Jersey, hunted moose and woodcock, raised hunting dogs and managed to fit in some tournament casting on summer Sundays.

The Paterson Casting Club met at the Oldham Pond near our home in North Haledon, and when the older of my two brothers, Jimmy, reached the age of eight, he went along with Dad to the club's practice sessions. Joan, who was ten, was bypassed.

I *wanted* to fly cast. Gaining Mom's permission to try it with Dad's fly rod one afternoon, I went to the casting club dock, put the rod together and flailed away. *Oops!* The tip and butt sections separated, and with no fly on the leader to stop it, the tip went into the six-foot-deep pond water. Home I went, crying and afraid of my father's anger. Mom may have been, too, because when our next-door neighbor came home from work, an hour before Dad would come in for dinner, she asked for his help. We went back to the dock with a garden rake and, bless Mr. Kuehn, he snagged it in a few minutes.

The dad I didn't know very well, the authoritarian figure in my life, the man of whom I was a little bit afraid, asked me to join him and Jimmy the next Sunday at the casting club.

I can look back now and say I was born to fly cast. While it wasn't easy, I was drawn to it. That same year (1937) a friend, Eleanor Egg, had talked my parents into letting me take tap, ballet and acrobatic lessons from her. I am convinced that the dancing lessons improved my casting because they taught me to use my whole body to back up my limited ten-year-old strength.

Casting and dancing became my favorite pastimes. I won my first casting title in 1938, the New Jersey Sub-Junior All Around

Championship, and with it gained the motivation to practice. Although I took college preparatory courses in high school, when my guidance counselor asked what my plans were ("I don't know") and what I liked to do ("fly cast and dance"), she suggested secretarial school.

I had started to teach tap dancing when I was thirteen, and by the time I took my first job as a junior secretary with N. W. Ayer & Sons, an advertising agency in New York City, for twenty-five dollars per week, I was earning twenty dollars for teaching dancing on Saturdays. Just before I turned eighteen I gave up secretarial work for dancing and opened a school with Eleanor. How lucky I was! She instilled in me the joy of living, and of teaching, and we had a perfect partnership for eight years. I taught dancing for ten months of the year and competed as an amateur in five or six casting tournaments during the two summer months.

Between 1943 and 1951 I won one or more national women's titles every year and, in 1951, garnered four, plus a fisherman's distance fly event against all-male competition. I beat the second-place winner—my boyfriend, Johnny Dieckman—by an average of one-third of a foot! This was an event in which I could master the tackle as well as the men because it was limited to what we now call a 9-weight line.

Distance fly casting had become my real love in tournaments. There were two distance fly events, the one mentioned above, with tackle suitable for actual fishing, and a second, the "unrestricted" trout fly event, with specialty tackle capable of making casts so long as to be impractical for a fisherman. The event, which is still included in casting competitions, challenges casters to design tackle and develop techniques to cast a fly as far as is humanly possible with a one-handed rod. Interestingly, the average fly angler does benefit. The shooting-head line and the double-haul casting technique were either developed or refined through tournaments.

I had begun by "ghillying" for my casting mentor, William Taylor. After each cast I pulled the dozens of yards of shooting line back in from the water and spread them out on the dock beside him. I came to appreciate that distance fly casting was a sport of beautiful form and motion, requiring the use of the whole body. In 1947 I could no longer resist trying it, but I found Bill's tackle too heavy, and so he made a lighter rod for me. Lighter? It weighed 6¾ ounces! (We had only bamboo to use then.)

For distance fly casting the silk line was specially constructed, by hand, of spliced sections of line of different diameter to form a taper. This tapered "head" was approximately fifty-two feet long and had a weight limitation of 1½ ounces. It was backed by monofilament shooting line and the record casts were 150 feet and up. I could not cast a line that heavy, so, once again, Bill Taylor made me a "lighter" one. It weighted 1⅜ ounces.

Even at those weights I could not false cast the outfit. I didn't have the strength to maintain line speed on a false cast, so all of my distance casting was done by taking the line off the water (with the head out of the rod tip), shooting on the backcast, and shooting the rest on the forward cast. In spite of my lack of strength, my coordination and timing allowed me to place about halfway down the line among the male competitors in most tournaments.

The longest cast I ever made in a national tournament was 144 feet, but in a registered New Jersey state tournament in 1960 I cast my fly 161 feet for an unofficial women's record. Unofficial because there weren't any, or enough, other women distance casters to have an event of our own. The men's record was less than 190 feet. Oh, that I could do it all again with graphite!

In 1948 fly casting brought me to the attention of angler, author and famous hotelier Charles Ritz at a sportsmen's show in New York. Charles invited me to compete in the French National Tournament in Paris and in the International Casting Tournament in London, the first events of their kind to be held after the war. I won the international ⅝-ounce plug-casting championship, competing against men and women, professionals and amateurs.

Our dancing school, meanwhile, had become very successful. In 1952 I decided to leave, with Eleanor's blessing, after realizing that if I didn't make a conscious break, I might be there for the rest of my life. That would mean I would always miss spring trout fishing because of preparations for our June dance recital.

Making a living in the sport-fishing field was next to impossible in those days, but sportsmen's show exhibitions were available to me, and the Ashaway Line and Twine Company hired me to do part-time goodwill work, calling on their dealers. In 1954 I did a series of shows in the Midwest with Monte Blue, star of the silent screen, as emcee. When I showed up in my shorts, hip boots and creel, which was everyone's idea of a girl fisherman's costume, Monte took me aside and told me he wanted to try something different. "Wear a dress," he said, "a long one, and we'll wow 'em." Leaping at the chance to portray casting as feminine, I bought a strapless, ankle-length white dress with silver leaves on it, high-heeled sandals and, to complete the outfit, rhinestones for my hair.

The combination was perfect and Monte presented my act beautifully, speaking softly, while I was casting, of grace, timing and beauty. I didn't cast at targets but, instead, used one rod and then two, creating as many interesting patterns with the fly lines as I could in time with the music. *Up a Lazy River* was a natural, and the audiences responded. It couldn't last forever, though, and without either Monte or an orchestra the costume didn't play as well mixed in with lumberjacks, retrievers and Sparky the seal. I changed back to the shorts, boots and creel outfit—but I'll remember the gown and music as being the perfect way to depict fly casting as an art form, especially suitable for women.

So there I was, a young woman in a man's field, gaining notoriety because of it, and feeling I was where I wanted to be. I had lots to learn; my fishing experience was broad but shallow. My generation of young women did not venture alone into the woods or streams. There were also the difficulties of the costume for stream fishing, and the discomforts of biting insects and bad weather. The gear, in a man's size small, was uncomfortable, and "bug dope," as it was called, was greasy and strong smelling. Because I loved being outdoors, I thought of it as paying the price to get the rewards, but I did not fish as often or as comfortably as a young man my age might have done. There have been remarkable advances in the area of comfort, for both men and women, in the last fifteen years.

In 1959, married and with one child, I took a part-time job with the Garcia Corporation, which was, then, the largest tackle company in the world. I lived in Florida at the time but my job was to promote their products, through clinics and exhibitions, anywhere in the country. Part of the job was to fish in tournaments, and that was a real bonus. Just like any other woman, juggling a career and a family left little time for recreational fishing.

Years later, as part of my work, I had the opportunity to appear in a film on giant bluefin-tuna fishing that Lee Wulff was producing for ABC's *American Sportsman* television series. Although Lee and I knew each other casually, it was our first opportunity to fish together. After our marriage in 1967, my fishing horizons expanded. We traveled to the West for trout, to the Canadian Maritime Provinces and Iceland for Atlantic salmon, and to Ecuador for marlin. We became a team for Garcia and held fly-fishing clinics and programs for clubs throughout the country.

My presence attracted women to these events. In earlier generations, men had gone on fishing trips partly to "get away from the wife," but now fishermen asked me to direct my words to their wives or girlfriends, hoping to convert them into companions who could share the pleasures of fly fishing. In 1979, Lee and I opened a fly-fishing school in New York's Catskill Mountains. Soon one-quarter of our students were women, and that percentage has now risen to one-third.

It is estimated that there are two million committed fly fishermen in the United States. Only ten percent of those, two hundred thousand or less, subscribe to the fly-fishing magazines, and readership is reported as ninety-six percent male. If as many as fifty or sixty percent of those male readers shares life with a woman, there is a great potential to swell our ranks. The greater the number of fly fisherwomen, the more likely it is that the manufacturers of equipment will cater to our special needs.

It has taken all of my life for the changes to develop in equipment and attitude that now make fly fishing a natural extension of a woman's love of the outdoors. Whether you are married to a fisherman or are a single woman, there is nothing to stop you now except lack of time. Fortunately, one of the strengths of our sex is our high tolerance for interruption.

Recently, artist Phyllis Sheffield, a friend who shares my love of dancing but who fishes only casually, listened patiently while I bubbled on about a recent fishing trip. "Joanie," she asked, "don't you *ever* get tired of fishing?" "No," I replied, "because it is always renewing!"

Sure, I can have enough of fishing on a tough day or in circumstances that are particularly uncomfortable, but I will never tire of what fishing gives me. It puts me in touch with another of nature's species, in beautiful surroundings that are as old as time. That is where I want to be; that is how I am renewed.

JUDY MULLER

Only One Fly?

ONE OF THE reasons I love
to fly fish is the relaxing rhythm of the sport—the total removal,
in place and purpose, from the stress and competition of work. So
when I was asked to participate in the Jackson Hole One-Fly contest, my first concern was that competing in the sport might nul-
lify its healing powers. My second concern was that I wouldn't be
as good as the other contestants. In other words, I was already
competing. But the official literature for the contest insisted this
would be a different sort of competition: *While some fly fisherman may find the idea of competitive fly fishing repugnant and
against what fly fishing is all about, let us point out that this is a
friendly competition.*

"Friendly." Sounded reassuring enough. And I admit I needed all the reassurance I could get; after agreeing to fish on one of the thirty-two teams in the One-Fly, all the insecurities about my fishing ability came roiling to the surface, like so many trout on a feeding frenzy—the so many trout that, over the years, had ignored so many of my attempts to "match the hatch" of insects on the water with just the right artificial fly.

But in this event, there would be no "matching the hatch." The great equalizer in the One-Fly is just that: ONE FLY. Each angler is allowed only one fly for each day of the competition; the four anglers on each team do not have to use the same fly. All 144 contestants face the same daunting problem: once you have lost that fly, be it a Double Humpy, a Royal Wulff or a Madame X, to any obstacle, be it a tree, a rock or even a fish, you are out of the competition for the day. You may continue to fish, but the trout you catch won't count on your team's score, which is based on the number and size of the fish you hook.

Now there is not a fly fisherman on earth, no matter how skilled, who has not been humbled by a low-hanging branch or a submerged boulder. Depending on the difficulty of retrieval, an angler often chooses to snap off the fly and tie on a new one. In the One-Fly, however, contestants and their official guides go to great lengths to retrieve that one precious fly, even to the point of bringing along pruning shears and saws, not to mention snorkels and masks. But more on that later.

The One-Fly, an invitational event put on annually by the One-Fly Foundation in Jackson, Wyoming, and is designed to promote conservation projects, including catch-and-release fishing. In the contest, barbless hooks are mandatory, since they do less damage to the fish and speed up the process of getting the fish back in the water. Any fish deemed mortally wounded by the judges results in penalty points for the contestant. I bring this up because it is crucial to the moral of our story.

I had been invited to participate in the One-Fly by Silvio Calabi, the editor of *Fly Rod and Reel* magazine. He had put together a team of four journalists (the Journos), but by the time contest-day arrived, two members had dropped out. We filled in the blanks with two fishermen on the alternate list: David Kern, senior vice president of Zebco Tackle, and John Garrison, a thirty-six-year old from Knoxville, who introduced himself as a doctor and a member of the Tennessee House of Representatives. At the Jackson Hole restaurant where the team gathered for a get-acquainted dinner, Garrison told me an intriguing story about working undercover for the Drug Enforcement Agency, work that had resulted, he said, in threats on his life. As we left the restaurant, Calabi whispered to me, "I'll bet there's more to this guy than meets the eye." *Much* more, actually.

I had arrived in Jackson Hole two days before the competition to have a chance to fish for the native cutthroat trout without the pressure of cutthroat competition. And so I had a delightful day fishing on the meandering Snake River, learning the way the trout strike (fast, with *no* slack allowed in the line) and where they tend to feed (near the banks, naturally, under fly-eating trees). The weather was sunny and mild, the Tetons a dramatic backdrop. But the weather was about to make a dramatic change, dropping the curtain on those mountains and, for that matter, on the entire Jackson Hole valley.

At the cocktail party on the eve of the contest, weather was one of the main topics of conversation. If it rained, we wondered, would a wet fly, fished underneath the surface, work better than a dry fly fished on top? If it snowed, someone asked, as it had two years earlier, would the fish be feeding at all? (*Snow?* I had just flown in from L.A., where *rain* leads the evening news. *Snow?*)

Any way you cut it, this was not your ordinary cocktail chatter. "A Humpy? Nah, I'd bet on a Madame X." "Try a muddler or something with rubber legs." All around the room, the question of *which fly* was being discussed in conspiratorial tones by contestants ranging from the governor of Wyoming to sportscaster Curt Gowdy. There was also some speculation (at least among the men) about whether the rain would prevent actress Heather Thomas from fishing in a swimsuit this year. (It would.)

Scott Sanchez, a local fly tier known for his ability to create "bomb-proof" flies for this event, was working the room like a drug dealer, dispensing special-ordered flies from a small box. I was among those waiting to buy. I had ordered a couple of Royal Trudes, a fly that can be fished wet or dry. In a field of contestants that included expert guides from New Zealand and casting champion Joan Wulff, I figured I would need all the help I could get.

I awoke at six the next morning to the sound of rain. Groan. We all met at Nellie's, a local restaurant, for breakfast and pairing up with guides. Each guide was to act as judge (monitoring our flies and measuring our catch) and boatman for two contestants from different teams. We would fish from 8:30 A.M. to 4:30 P.M., with a break for lunch, on various assigned stretches of the Snake. Before leaving for our stretch, called, ominously enough, "Deadman's," a local guide said to me, "Don't worry about which fly you choose. It's not the fly that counts; it's how it's fished." I think he actually believed this would make me feel better.

My fishing partner that first day was Terry Collier of the Utah Trout Foundation team. Terry, a professional fishing guide by trade, told me he was "just here to have a good time." He did appear to be exceptionally relaxed about the whole thing. As we drove to our put-in point, Collier asked our guide, Bob Lowe, about a fly sitting on his dashboard, gathering dust. "Oh, that's a Letort Hopper with rubber legs," replied Lowe. Collier decided he liked the looks of it and would use it in the competition. After all my angst about which fly to use, this guy picks up an old fly off someone's dashboard! I concluded there was probably a lot to this "it's not the fly but how you fish it" business.

As Lowe put the boat in the water, I tied on my trusty Trude with a knot of Gordian proportions. I used a 3X leader, one of the strongest available. No doubt the fish would see it attached to the fly and not be fooled for an instant, but I was taking no chances on losing my fly before noon. As luck would have it, I started out in the front of the boat (contest rules call for changing places at midday), with first shot at the good pools. As skill would have it, that didn't make much difference. About twenty feet from the put-in point, I made a cast to the left bank, let the fly float under an overhanging tree and congratulated myself on just the right mixture of caution and daring. After picking up my fly to cast forward again, I glanced back to see Collier try the same place with his Hopper. *Bam!* He pulled out a twenty-inch cutthroat. Lowe measured it, I took its picture, and Collier released it into the water. At that point, I became acutely aware that my hip waders, when I was in a sitting position, did not meet my rain jacket and that my lap was soaking wet. It was 8:35 A.M. This could be a very long day.

But while it was a very wet and very cold day, it never dragged. Only my line did that. As the day went on, however, my casting improved, and I managed to catch four fish by early afternoon. Because they were nowhere near as big as the four that Collier had caught, my score was nowhere near as high. But it didn't matter. I was pleased to be on the scoreboard at all, so sure had I been that I would lose my fly in the first half hour. Actually, I didn't lose it until 2:30 P.M., and then it was in the most honorable of ways, to a fat fifteen-inch cutthroat. The fly broke off in his mouth, and he was gone. And so was my anxiety. Free to fish without concern for the score, I began to catch more fish (I'm sure there's a lesson in there somewhere).

Collier's Hopper had by this time lost two of its four rubber legs. Even on its last legs, it was still doing the job for him. But he, too, finally lost his fly to a big fish, and we were in the same boat, literally and figuratively, for the last couple of hours. It was nice to focus on something other than the relentless casting, for a change. We saw otters, eagles, a male elk bugling for its mate, and an osprey latching on to a trout with its talons and flying off. No catch-and-release fishing for him.

Back at the bar at Nellie's, folks were clearly glad to be out of the rain and wasted no time swapping stories. One poor fellow had lost his fly on the third cast, while another, who had managed to keep his fly, caught nothing but a cold. Certain teams began to emerge as the ones to watch. Team Sage (of Sage Rods company) was reported to have caught a number of big fish, as had the Hollywood All-Stars, a team that included the aforementioned actress and her significant other, attorney Skip Brittenham, a member of the U.S. team in the 1989 world fly-fishing championships. Our team had acquitted itself well, thanks to the efforts of team captain Calabi and Garrison, the mysterious "alternate" from Tennessee.

That night at the banquet at Teton Pines, most conversations began with "How'd you do?" followed by "Where'd you go?" and "What'd you use?" Since anglers are allowed to change flies on the second day, there was a lot of curiosity about which flies had been most successful the first day. Apparently the Trude was one of them. I decided to stick with it.

Day Two dawned cold and cloudy, but since it wasn't raining, the optimists at breakfast were saying, "Looks like it might clear up! Could be worse!" It didn't and it could. The minute we hit the river, the rain came down in buckets, much worse than anything we had seen the previous day. This time, I was prepared. I had borrowed long, warm neoprene waders and was layered in a sweater and two jackets. I looked like a fat chocolate bunny. I didn't care.

On this day, I was paired up with Mike Atwell of the Sage Team. Our guide was Bob Barlow, a local lad who had come prepared with saw and snorkel for fly retrievals of heroic proportions. He also came prepared with a backup rod, and a good thing, too. I'd been having trouble with my four-piece rod fitting together properly and, sure enough, it cracked on a cast in the middle of the day.

Atwell was using a fly called a Stimulator, which not only sounded obscene but also caught an obscene number of fish. About ten fish to each one of mine, in fact. But I bettered my own score from the day before and even managed to catch a couple of small brown trout, something of a rarity on this stretch of the Snake. Our assigned beat was the Canyon, a deep ravine with many sections of raging white water. The fishing was difficult, requiring rapid, accurate casting to pockets along the bank. We passed a number of One-Flyers who'd become snagged on rocks and trees. And one group, deciding to fish from the bank for a while, watched in despair as their raft got loose and took off downstream without them.

In the last two hours of competition, we were visited by torrential downpours, lightning and thunder. When one optimist called out the predictable "Well, it could be worse," it began to hail. At any rate, everyone was more than ready to call it a day and head for the wrap-up awards barbecue.

I had managed to hang on to my fly for the entire day and caught a respectable number of fish. And I knew I had conquered the "competition thing" when I had to ask the guide just how many fish. Nine, he said, for a total of forty points (seventy-two for the two days). Other members of my team covered the whole range of fortune. David Kern lost his fly early in the day, Calabi brought in 137 points, while Garrison wowed everyone with a total of 345 points. He also believed he had landed what surely must have been the big fish of the contest, a twenty-three inch cutthroat. He caught it on a fly he had tied himself, a version of a Double Humpy he called a Double-Breasted Mattress Thrasher (even fly fishing has its "bubba" factor).

At the barbecue, tales of valiant fly retrievals abounded. One woman reportedly swam under her boat, emerging on the other side with rod and fly intact. A guide from New Zealand was forced to go out on a limb, literally, to retrieve his fly, snagged in the branches of a wobbly lodgepole pine. And another angler reported leaving footprints on the shoulders of his guide, after using him as a ladder to reach the uppermost branches of a tree.

The winning team: the Hollywood All-Stars, with Skip Brittenham the "high hook" at 401 points. We ranked ninth out of thirty-six, because of the efforts of Garrison. As for his big fish, it became something of a cause célèbre. At the awards banquet, the president of the One-Fly contest committee, announced there had been a bit of a glitch with Garrison's catch: it seems the fish was never measured by the guide. When Garrison hooked his twenty-three-incher, he was on the bank far upstream from the guide. Fearing that his fish would die before the guide got to him,

Garrison held up the fish for the guide to see, then marked the length of the trout on his fly rod and released his catch back into the water. Because "rules are rules," he said, the official record would go to a twenty-two-inch trout caught by someone else. But because catch-and-release and good sportsmanship are what the One-Fly is all about, added the president, Garrison would also receive a trophy.

A nice story, right? And that's right where I would have ended it, had I not learned more about our mysterious teammate weeks later, after he was arrested on a drunken-driving charge by the Jackson Hole police. They discovered that Garrison was wanted in Knoxville on theft and forgery charges. He was returned to Tennessee, where he pleaded guilty to theft. According to investigators, he was neither a doctor nor a member of the state legislature, though he had official-looking plates on his car. Police suspect he was using the One-Fly as an entree to the Jackson Hole social scene and some *really* big fish. We may never know the truth about all the stories he told us. What's unusual about this fish story, in fact, is that the only thing we know for sure is the size of the fish he caught. Then again . . .

SALLY I. STONER

Women in the Stream

MENOPAUSE WAS a cruel slap. All winter she wrestled each tentacle of its symptoms, like a scuba diver in a low-budget, underwater horror movie, slashing at a giant octopus, bubbles rising to the roof of the cave, her arms and legs flailing wildly, while the grisly appendages wrapped around her in unrelenting coils.

A day would start out in optimistic promise and end with a blinding migraine. In a flash, friendly conversations disintegrated into emotional confrontation. Simple tasks, usually performed without a thought, became incomprehensible. Food ruled her. She pandered to carbohydrates, whored wantonly to simple sugars.

The behavior distortions were the hardest. "Mood swings" were a good name for the experience. As if on a ride on the playground of middle age, she swung—from high to low, loving to evil, compassionate to homicidal. Maybe she would get the estrogen patch. All her friends and co-workers were lobbying for some hormonal panacea. Whatever it took for respite from the swings.

Lately, people approached her with quizzical expressions on their faces, the most courageous of her friends finding it best to ask what her mood was if the air around her looked smoky. They had learned the hard way that a fire-breathing beast could emerge unexpectedly and singe their hair.

The worst tentacle of the monster was the homicidal streak, which appeared randomly and was beyond her control. When held in its grasp, she knew for certain that she could kill without remorse. She planned her murders in the long, dark hours after midnight when hot flashes made sleep impossible. The weapon was a shotgun—no aiming necessary at close range. The victims were usually short men whose smug little grins were wiped off their faces at the sight of two gleaming barrels.

During a memorable late-night rampage she planned her boss' punishment after he lowered her performance review. He fit the profile of her typical prey: short and smug. His mistake was shoving her ability into the constraints of a bell curve. He had pushed her score backward into the mediocre hump to meet his quota, decreasing her raise and committing the unforgivable act of diminishing her ability in order to satisfy his budget statistic. Now he must pay the price, another victim of the menopausal murderess.

The scenario took deliberate, sequential steps. It would be slow. Torture was necessary. She held him hostage in his second-floor office. While the SWAT team gathered, she nipped off small pieces of his anatomy. Bit by bit. A part here, a tuft there, until he was insane with terror. She would teach him the lesson of his own soulless inhumanity. When it was over and the police slapped the cuffs on her, she would be the one with the smug grin. Without repentance she'd accept her sentence.

"Big deal," she thought. "So they send me to prison. Three hots and a cot. A simple cotton shift and jelly sandals to wear. Full medical benefits and big-boned dykes to watch over me. At least I'll be in a society of women."

It was another long, sleepless night. She went to work the next morning still mean and cranky, and it took days for her mood to swing back to a lighter side.

Her best medicine during the long winter months is the photo on her desk. It had been taken last summer to commemorate three great days spent fly fishing on the Deschutes River. It is a group portrait. Nine women bedraggled but smiling. Short, tall, chunky, and slim, all wearing their look-alike shirts. All except Effie, who in her packing frenzy had forgotten to include the *one* item she had been reminded to bring, the royal blue Lands' End with a rising trout and "Deschutes 1992" embroidered in white over the pocket.

The women are posed among the drift boats, with the Deschutes flowing in the background. Now the memory of the adventure quiets the maniac inside her. During those three days they had made lifetime memories. She loses herself inside the snapshot whenever the present becomes overwhelming. She calls it "Women in the Stream," and it is her hormone therapy. Sometimes she toys with the idea of taping the snapshot to her behind: "I wonder if my system could absorb this medicine. Seems like it would be better for me than Premarin."

When this summer arrives, she'll slip on her L. L. Bean fluffies, squeeze into blue neoprene waders, and load her vest with fly boxes, tippet, leader, split shot and chocolate chip granola bars. She will begin the mental preparation for her fishing trip by visualizing the feel of the graphite rod loaded with line. She imagines the cast. Her mind's eye sees her fly landing on the river's surface. She knows her first attempts will be rusty and oafish. She doesn't mind. It is the process that subdues the monster. The image that cools the heat. This summer she will share the Madison River with her friends. Buoyed by anticipation and the knowledge that neither estrogen patch nor vitamin therapy is required to drift a nymph past a feeding trout, she imagines their enthusiastic faces reflected in the Madison. She looks forward to the late evenings spent sharing the day, planning the next, and comparing battles with the monster. That's real therapy. It helps her spirit soar beyond the madness of middle life.

June begins a new season on the Madison River. The first morning of her visit she walks along Highway 287 and over the bridge crossing Cabin Creek. She carries her rod sections in her left hand. Her cocker spaniel trots happily in front, breaking an invisible trail. Old routines come easily out of winter storage, and memories walk beside her.

Her personal journey has taken her many places. She has always traveled with fishing tackle and has wet her line in a hundred wonderful pools. She waited until her thirties to give herself up to angling with fly and soon realized the sport was almost exclusively the realm of men. Browsing through tackle shops, she noticed immediately that she became invisible, at least while she looked through the fly patterns, but once she crossed the unmarked line into the clothing section, she would suddenly materialize and the shopkeeper would descend upon her. Apparently, after ignoring her presence among the tackle, where she didn't belong, he thought he would ring up a big ticket sale in Patagonia labels. Or even more insulting, he would ask if she was looking for a gift for her husband. It was always a surprise to him when she would respond with a laugh and promptly exit the store.

It became a game. She would walk into a shop and ease her way around the displays, making mental notes of the location where she was discovered. Sometimes, she circled the entire shop without ever being acknowledged, doomed to be the invisible patron. Usually, she spent at least fifty dollars in a fly shop. Most visits had the potential to cost her much more, if only the shopkeeper would wait on her. "Oh well," she'd think as she left, "another schmoe in the retail trade."

She would head up the road with her traveler's checks unsigned, relaying as much negative advertising about the experience as she could. She refused to join the conspiracy of silence. On the contrary, she tattled freely on bad behavior or unprofessionalism among guides, shops and resorts. Hoping other women would not suffer the same indignities, she spread the word as best she could. She even penned a few letters to the sport magazines, just in case there were any women readers. The unpleasant were crossed off her list permanently along with places where she was treated with disdain or sanctimony. Generally the worst offenders were gone by the following season. One particularly odious shop owned by a fellow she called "the weasel" actually burned to the ground one winter. For that she took no credit. The demise of errant shops was unmourned, but duly noted.

Is it menopause causing her to be more critical? The mid-life imbalances that make the bitter pill harder to swallow?

Diminishing estrogen being replaced with increased testosterone. That's one theory. If it is "the change" decreasing her tolerance for sexist behavior, she welcomes it. She is fed up with second-class treatment and quiet acceptance of prejudice.

She returns to the present time as the river comes into full view. The sight of the river always stuns her. Her cocker seems to feel the same way: he can be asleep in the back of the van, but as soon as the road parallels a river, he wakes instantly and leaps into the front seat, panting and wagging his tail in anticipation. She, too, feels like panting and wagging her tail. Instead, she takes in a long, deep breath and exhales with a slow sigh.

She reaches the edge of the Madison and climbs down the bank to a spot they call "The Flats." Finding a dry boulder, she perches to assemble her gear. The cocker runs off sniffing for squirrels, his cropped tail wildly wagging.

Before focusing on her gear she sits very still to watch and listen. She frees all her senses, for immersing herself in the surroundings. Overhead large cumulus clouds float in a crisp blue sky, and across the river cedars still drip from last night's rain. The river flows high and clear. Below the clouds and just above tree line, the osprey and pelican soar. A pair of mergansers swim easily in a smooth pond behind a fallen log. White field lilies stand erect. Fresh moose tracks trot along the river's edge. She feels no evil tentacles here.

She thinks back on last year's trip. Nine women fishing and floating the Deschutes River. It had started as one of her great ideas. A flash along the lines of "I know, kids, let's build a stage in the old barn and put on a show." Except her burst of brilliance was to gather a group of women for a fishing expedition, a float trip down some of Oregon's best waters in drift boats loaded with estrogen.

She had spent months planning, organizing and talking with the outfitter about the eating habits of women. It would have been great to organize a totally female tour including outfitter, guides, cook and baggage-boat rower, but she had not been aware of an all-women guide service. Besides, she had been reluctant to do this trip with an untested infrastructure. Her flimsy nerves could not handle surprises.

The guide she chose had his share of warts, but she had fished with him in the past and felt his quirks were acceptable. Meals might be the only problem. He regaled his male clientele with truckloads of food, mostly beast parts and mounds of carbohydrates. Not palatable menus for her group. When she broached the subject, his response had been, "The food is the *only* thing I can control. Not the weather or the fishing. Just the food." Mr. Guide was an old-timer on the Deschutes, having rowed and fished the river for more than thirty years.

She wanted this trip to be an opportunity for the group to be together. Most of them were traveling without their husbands or partners and would have the chance to be who they were as a solo act. Their only common objective was to entice rainbow trout to rise to their imitation insects. Beyond that end, the trip offered many "firsts." The first vacation with other women, the first fishing trip, the first camping trip, the first guided adventure with men waiting on you hand and foot, the first trip without a shower—the list seemed endless and the possibilities abundant. It was a chance to enjoy a beautiful river and all that lived in and with it. To be part of the current during the day and to sleep in its song by night. A journey of discovery for all of them.

The nine who made the commitment were a good mix of rookies and seasoned anglers, lesbians and straights, the young and not so young, the serious as well as the lighthearted, mothers and the childless, teetotalers and imbibers, the functional and the neurotic. Astrologically, they were overloaded with earth signs, cardinal, fixed and immutable. There were a couple of fire signs to boss them around, and two Pisces whose shared birthday occurred on the final day of the sign so that one was a suspected Aries.

She shared her menopausal condition with Effie, who, although a few years older, was also wrestling the octopus. Her comrade in mid-lifery was her opposite in most personality traits. Together they were fighting the night demons, hot flashes and mood changes. Her steady friend, always the even-tempered voice of reason, was now an alien host-body. That amused her. She felt Effie was too accommodating and it was high time she spoke up in discord.

"After a few sleepless nights, I didn't seem to care if my husband ever touched me again. It was just the strangest feeling," Effie reported during one of their discussions.

They were patients of the same nurse practitioner, who, as it happened, was also going through menopause. They noticed their medicine woman was adapting her clinical advice to her own current symptoms. Now that the change was a personal reality to her, she had thrown away her book of traditional remedies in favor of any treatment that could actually calm the octopus. All three of them were wondering who would try the patch first. Their nurse confided during one gyno-visit that she couldn't bear to add anything else to her body. She said she felt much too lumpy already.

It was good to have a comrade in menopause. The trial needed as much informational exchange as possible. Her mother, when living, had never offered to lift the veil from the mystery. She remembered her mother as being wacky, but there had been many reasons for her peculiar behavior and being an adolescent at the time, she had ignored her mother's insanity. Effie was reading every piece of information she could find on the subject. It didn't matter if it was *The Readers Digest* or the *New Witches Review*. She read it and reported on it. The river trip would be a good time to review the latest literature.

The group assembled in the tiny town of Madras the night before "put-in" to meet Mr. Guide and organize the gear. After dinner she gave them a safety lecture on river hazards, snakes, stinging insects, hypothermia and lightning. This was followed by a demonstration of basic knot tying. Finally, she and her companion, the Aries, did gear inventory. They culled unnecessary clothing, accessories and hair dryers from the group's duffels. They would camp two nights on the river, where there was no access to electricity, and waders were the uniform of the day. Silly women. Her menopause buddy tried to sneak a curling iron back into her Pierre Cardin bag.

"Look, Effie, it's bad enough you've got this fancy damn luggage, but the hot curlers are definitely out."

"Well, what about Cindy? She still has her pager on, and she's reading *Re-engineering the Corporation* in hardback."

"I know. I just caught her trying to call her secretary on her cell-phone. But she's your tent buddy. You deal with her. I gave up years ago."

No one slept well, and by 4:00 A.M. the Aries had awakened everyone with hot coffee and her infectious smile. Before the morning heated up the group crammed butts and elbows into the van and headed for the river. By seven o'clock three drift boats were bobbing down the Deschutes River loaded to the gunwales with women, fly rods, day packs and anticipation. A year of planning and agonizing launched at last.

"Now," she thought, "they're on their own. I've got them to the water. The rest is up to them."

The first fish was hooked and landed by a rookie wearing "Gladbag" look-alikes for waders. The novice angler nearly jumped out of her plastic trousers as the trout went aerial after her elk hair caddis. She hollered with joy while playing her first fish and danced delightedly during the entire struggle. Ms. Gladbags was a first-time angler who had begged to be included in the group. There she was catching the first trout of the trip only ten minutes after put-in. As the other boats drifted past the happy angler, all hands shouted encouragement and waved like fools.

Word of the all-women float spread along the river. Nights between fishing trips must be especially long and lonely for guides in small Oregon towns. So this information was considered news. The other outfitters clucked their tongues and felt sorry for the hapless guides stuck with the female trip. When they rowed past, their voices could be heard above the song of the river: "It's those daggone women. He's got 'em in all the best spots."

As luck would have it, one of the women usually hooked a whopper at the precise moment a boatload of guys slipped past. Oddly, the boys never saluted the hook-up with a cheer. Nope, they would turn their eyes downriver and row like hell to get away from such a gruesome sight. The other women would taunt their fleeing compatriots by yelling to each other about the size of the trout and what a great fight it was putting up. Afterward, the lucky fisherwomen said a grateful prayer to the Trout Goddess for the fortuitous catch while their boatboys pumped up their chests pridefully and mentally took all the credit.

The hot day flew by as the women learned to cast a fly with accuracy. They were instructed on the merits of a drag-free float and became adept at mending a slack line. They felt the exhilaration of a singing reel, a bowed rod and a leaping red-sided trout. They suffered the brow-beating of a fuss-budget Mr. Guide for eating way too little, having their first cup of coffee inside their tents, and being careless with the zippers on the tent flaps. Mr. Guide was very cranky. Ms. Gladbags drank a slosh of wine every evening and coquettishly engaged the youngest of the row-boys. Ms. Corporate finally put down her book and joined the group in more earthy conversation. The elder members told the stories of their lives and listened patiently to the youngsters. The menopausal buddies talked of herbal estrogen, vaginal dryness and other hideous tentacles of the monster.

During a slow afternoon on the second day, six women were fishing in the same section. The boatboys lounged together out of earshot smoking. Five of the women gave up fishing to languish in the shade. The most diligent of the group continued to cast to visible trout without much luck. The lazies perched easily on the trunk and watched their dedicated sister bend forward to coax the swimming trout to her fly.

The devil possessed the Aries, and she tossed a small pebble in front of the fishing woman. When the tiny splash erupted, she called to her friend to cast to the rise. Ms. Angler whirled in the direction of the splash and whipped her line like mad to where she thought the fish broke the surface. Ms. Aries, still bedeviled, chucked a pebble and yelled again. Ms. Angler turned to cast to the ripple. The women on the log were shaking with stuffed-down laughs. After the fourth or fifth pebble rise, Ms. Angler finally saw the rock hit the water. She about-faced and ran through knee-deep water straight for the Aries. Fire-snorting and wild-eyed, she grabbed Ms. Aries off the snag and down they went laughing and splashing. And so did the other women, who let go of their glee with such force that they all fell into the river. The young oarsmen looked over to the group of hysterical females in amazement. The boys scratched their heads while the women laughed until they thought they would wet themselves.

One of the best days was fishing with the two eldest members of the trip. The most senior was just reaching seventy and fished harder than anyone. It was not unusual to see her armpit-deep in the river making long elegant casts to working fish. But Ms. Senior never seemed to be bothered by the water. When asked if it didn't frighten her to wade so deeply, she responded, "Well, now that you mention it, no, it doesn't. There isn't much that scares me anymore."

The second in seniority was only sixty. Her patience and quiet diligence had paid dividends throughout her life and given her the edge in angling. She would wear the fish down. They would bite even if they weren't hungry out of sheer exhaustion. She had a tenacity of will that even worked on Mr. Guide. He was a pussy cat for her. At mealtime he would walk behind the diners threatening their heads with a spatula if they didn't eat ten more pancakes. But when he came to her, he would touch her gently on the shoulder and ask if he could take her plate. Groans would well up from the others as they tried to shove one more forkful into a reluctant mouth.

The last night on the river was bittersweet. The group was exhausted after two long, hard, hot days of concentrated fishing. Mr. Guide was busy cooking enough food to feed a small Caribbean country, while Ms. Gladbags was well on her way to sleaziness. There was an ideal spot for bathing about fifty yards upriver from the camp, a large flat rock nestled into a quiet back eddy and screened by willows from the main channel of the river. Some of the women left together and some alone. When the

Aries and she were certain that all of their charges had taken their turns, they went to refresh themselves.

Stripping off their shorts and tank tops in the warm evening air, they silently dipped cupped hands into the cool river water and began to wash. It was like stepping back to a time when women routinely bathed in the river. Like an ancient ritual it felt somehow sacred. They soaped and rinsed each other's back and shampooed one another's hair. When they finished, they sat on the bank letting the breeze dry their bodies. Walking back slowly to camp they shared a feeling of purification. Baptized.

After dinner the conversation around the campfire ranged from the innocence of adolescence and first intimacies through the mystery of parenting and Doris Day's sexual preference. The boys gathered at a discreet distance from the women, but kept their ears cocked toward the intriguing discussion. Wondering if their girlfriends had these odd chats, they exchanged confused glances and sipped their beers.

The women's talk shifted to the trip. It was clear everyone would not be best pals, but all agreed the float was unforgettable. The experience of fishing with remarkable women was not about how many fish were landed or who caught the biggest trout. It was an unusual adventure for them. It was laughing, grumbling, sloshing, casting, reeling, flirting, snoring, eating, belching and fishing together. An experience that begged to be repeated.

This summer on the Madison there would be no drift boats or cranky guides, but there would be women fishing together again. Her attention back on the Montana present, she begins to assemble her rod. Her fingers caress every surface: line guides, wraps, tip top, cork grip and metal reel rings. There's no wooden reel seat. Instead the cork has been patiently worked into a flat area just big enough for the Hardy reel. The rear foot slips under a metal holder, and the front edge secures with a knurled O ring. Balance, perfect balance. The rod was hand-crafted by Paul Brown, a 4-weight built to fish the Madison.

Once the sections of the nine-foot rod are aligned, she attaches the Hardy and spools off enough line to thread the guides. Doubling over the line, she runs it through each stainless steel loop.

How many times, hurrying to cast to rising fish, had she missed a critical loop? She would discover her error after making her first cast. Then, cussing like a sailor, she would bring in her line, remove the fly from the tippet, and restring her rod, this time checking each guide to be certain it held line. Usually trout were splashing wildly around her as she reworked the line. They taunted her with their brazen flight after caddis flies. She would be half crazed with anticipation before she was finally ready to offer the acrobatic *Salmonidae* her elk hair version of a caddis.

Today, there are no splashy rises, no caddis flies emerging. This morning is meant for dead-drifting nymphs. The guides loaded, she carefully ties on a new leader to her fly line. It's cold, the temperature hovering in the fifties. Age and injury are not kind to her finger joints. She concentrates hard to make them twist the monofilament into the proper configuration. When the ends are wrapped, the tangle of line goes into her mouth for wetting. Sufficiently lubricated, the ends are pulled together into a precise barrel knot.

Tying that particular knot always makes her exclaim, "Hah!" She isn't sure why. She just feels strong and self-reliant when she successfully ties a barrel knot. Someday, when her knuckles become big and too stiff to manipulate the leader properly, she'll use the loop system, a simpler connection. Until then, which she hopes to be twenty or thirty years hence, she considers loops for wussies.

"Hah!" she says out loud. Her companion looks over knowing exactly where she is in the tackle process. Next she goes to the right side-pocket of her vest to choose tippet. Looking again at the water for the flow rate, she does an obtuse, inexplicable formula in her cerebral cortex and choses a 4-weight tippet. The end tackle is tied to the leader with a double surgeon's knot, a name indicating a much more sophisticated entanglement than the reality of the tie. A bright-orange strike-indicator is threaded onto the leader. Maybe it is cheating to use one, but she knows she's missed many strikes without it. She would rather have the excitement of playing a big bow than the dubious glory of being a purist.

She removes her box of wet flies from her upper-left pocket. The organization of her vest is precise. She knows the order of pocket contents without thinking. Her hand can rip a Velcro tab and extract whatever's needed at the moment. Chapstick, tippet, bug spray, pliers, Kelly clamp, floatant or granola bar, even in a coma she'd know the location of every item.

She selects a red San Juan worm from her box, a new pattern among her collection. She's an admitted fly whore, never can have enough. Some are more than ten years old, but she can't bring herself to use them. Someone dear had tied them, or they are too beautiful to lose, feathery mementos of her many expeditions. She has many boxes full.

The fly pattern is secured to the tippet with a double clinch knot. It looks tasty and irresistible. Last, she pinches on a non-lead split shot twelve inches above the skinny, red worm-imitator.

Rod rigged she ties the cocker to a long lead. He will have to stay on the bank, the water is too high to swim him across to the island. She eases herself into the river. Wading requires all of her concentration. Each foot must be carefully planted before her weight is transferred. The current is very strong, and one mis-step is potentially fatal. Challenging the river with nonchalance is a fool's game.

Slowly she makes her way to the far side of the small island. There is an enticingly deep slick about fifteen feet from the shallows. She rests momentarily before she starts to work the water toward the slick, casting a bit further after each pickup. On the fifth cast her indicator hesitates for a nanosecond. She lifts the rod tip and her reel sings. Almost simultaneously, a three-pound rainbow trout breaks the surface in a magnificent leap.

Her heart drops into her waders and she lets out a yelp. This is the biggest trout she has ever hooked, and it is now taking all the line it can get. She is into her backing. It's a jet trout zooming to Ennis. The rod bends, the reel screams, the line like a razor rips the water—it's ecstasy.

She plays the big fish valiantly. The cocker bays loudly from the far shore encouraging her. She runs as far as she can downriver to recover some line, but the water is too high to get much distance. In an effort to slow the fish, she fingers the reel to increase the tension but, suddenly, the rod tip straightens and her line falls limply on the water.

Off. The jet fish is gone. She reels in her line slowly, despite the adrenaline pumping through her body and the howling cocker. Examining her tippet, she sees the frayed end and realizes her San Juan worm is still in the giant trout's lip. Within hours the enzymes in the trout's secretions will dissolve the hook completely. A small scar may mark the fish where their connection was made, but her recollection will last a lifetime.

She sits on the bank of the island to repair her tackle, her heart beating wildly, her hands shaking slightly. She's smiling a huge smile.

"Come on, octopus. Try to beat me now. No mid-life demon is a match for me."

As she ties on a fresh tippet, she discards the cheery idea of going to prison for murdering smug little men. After all, she might be in the company of women, but there are no trout streams within the confines of the penitentiary. Angling with fly is her lethal weapon against the menace of menopause. She tugs the knot securely to the eye of the hook, clips the tag end of the tippet away, and looks downriver. She feels triumphant.

In a few days, some of her fishing companions from the Deschutes trip will join her on the Madison. They'll create a legend on the river just by being there and being women. They'll go to the fly shops in West Yellowstone. They'll ask for PMDs and Sparkle Pupas without batting an eye and they'll tell fish stories in loud voices. Fishermen will recognize and greet them by saying, "You must be the women we heard about. Having any luck? What are you using?" They will fight the tentacles and slay the octopus. They will take their rightful place midstream.

ELIZABETH ARNOLD

Gurry

I T'S THREE IN the morning and I'm swimming in slimy, half-dead sockeye salmon. My gloved hands grip the bars above as I kick wildly, using my whole body to move thousands of pounds of fish toward a large, swinging hose. The vacuum sucks them up indiscriminately from the dark, stinking hold of this boat out onto the dock above.

The hold is a large, swaying, rusty metal cell. I grab on whenever I can, slipping and climbing in a waist-deep mixture of fish, blood and scales, trying to stay upright as I shove salmon toward the sucking hose. There's a high-pitched whine as a large king salmon gets stuck. My fingers in its palm-sized gills, I try to wrestle the fish free from the suction only to fall backwards into more fish. In the square of light above I see the tiny, bearded head of the skipper of this hunk of junk tender. He's pointing and laughing.

The water and fish recede as the hours go by. I'm exhausted, but down to the last few salmon, which I slide toward the hose, trying to stand in my water-filled waders on the slippery metal bottom of the hold. In the corner, there are four enormous kings, some rope, lead line, and an old boot, mistakenly or purposely buried in the midnight loads delivered by smaller boats to be brought aboard this tender.

It's July, and this is Bristol Bay, Alaska, home of the largest sockeye salmon run in the world. I've come to fish, but here I am on my knees, in the bowels of some old converted crabber.

These lifeless salmon are now my livelihood, somehow connected to the worm my brother smugly stuck on his hook long ago, when I could not bear to, and to the hours spent, years later, patiently learning to fly cast. Fishing, for some reason, has become my proving ground.

Alone and sunburned beside nameless streams, I've untangled my line again and again from overhanging branches. Alone and seasick in the stern of someone else's boat, I've untangled what seems like miles of gillnet. But when a single trout hits my convincing fly, or a dozen silver salmon sink my carefully placed driftnet, the sensation is the same. A silent but defiant, "I told you so," goes out to everyone and no one in particular.

It is that moment that has pulled me for miles along muddy trails and has kept me casting for hours with only scratches and mosquito bites to show for my effort. It is that moment that has pulled me away from graduation parties and job interviews to the bottom of this rusty boat in western Alaska.

Gurry

⌐∿

I gaff the last of the kings up to the deck above, then I too am hoisted out of the hold, clinging to the hose as it's lifted. All eyes are on the rushing tide. They're casting and coiling lines, heading back out for the fish that was caught as I slid and cursed below.

As the tender pulls away, I am making the prayerful leap from the rail to the dock ladder, avoiding a glimpse of the black water now forty feet below.

Forklift lights briefly illuminate the dock. I see Jill, balled up in her wet rain-gear, lying on a pile of pallets.

"You shouldn'ta let that big one through," she says, trying to light a soggy cigarette. "You could see it comin' up, like somethin' big stuck in your throat. Knocked the hell oughta me."

She's just finished sorting the fish that shot out of the other end of the hose onto the conveyor belt. The pace never slows. Eyes glued to the moving fish, the sorters focus on the tails. A flash of silver and a thick tail, it's a coho. Grab it quick, throw it into the one-ton tote filled with chipped ice on the left. Curled upper lip and purple watermarks, it's a dog; toss it into the tote marked "chum." No humpies in this load. And if it doesn't knock you over when it comes belching out of the hose, a king is easy to spot, big, with black speckles on its back and tail. But most of the fish are reds, sockeye salmon, left to run off the end of the belt into a tote on a waiting forklift that spins around leaving a trail of ice as it heads straight in to the slime line.

You can hear the grinder in there, already chewing up the guts of this load, heads and innards dropped to the floor by a dozen workers on the line, who clean fish after fish after fish.

Out here in the deep dark blue before dawn, I can now make out the rest of the sorters. They're sweeping up the dock, throwing fish eyeballs at each other, filling up more totes with ice for the next load.

It's best working outside. There's room to move around. You can see the sky and weather change. Jill and I had both worked inside on the slime line, hour after hour, slicing off heads, slitting the blood line, separating out the eggs. Nothing but the sound of the radio hanging from a hook in a plastic bag to break the monotony. But listening to the coded talk of fishermen doing what we wanted to be doing made it worse. Weary and nauseated, knives moving continuously, our eyes would meet across the bloody stainless steel table. We made a silent pact to get out.

Next we worked in the freezers, dipping the clean fish in icy brine tanks, laying them out on racks to be blast-frozen, then prying them back off and packing them into cardboard boxes labelled for Japan, Denver, New York. No slime or stink in the freezers, just damp cold. We layered long johns and all the clothes we had under our rain gear. Desperate, we put cayenne pepper in our steel-toed boots and rubber gloves. Our feet and hands turned orange red. We were still cold and wet, and we vowed again to get out.

It took endless hours on shifts no one wanted, but we *did* get out. Me first, then Jill, outside, out to the dock, closer to the boats and the fishing, out where we wanted to be.

After a while, no matter where you work in the cycle, you can't get away from the fish. Catch a five-minute rest in the locker room on a heap of wet rain-gear. Close your eyes, and you see fish. Fish tails, fish eyes, fish guts, fish mouths, fish. You talk about fish, you wait for the fish, you load and unload fish, you sort fish, you gut fish, you smell like fish, you dream about fish. Everything, but catch fish.

That's the bond between Jill and me. The unexplainable urge to catch fish. I hated her the night she arrived, drunk and bellowing. But like me, she left everything behind to get up here, and she was just as set as I was about fishing. In the darkened bunkroom she lit a cigarette, and I saw beside her duffle a fly rod and a Japanese egg box, which I discovered the next morning was filled with barbless hooks and well-tied flies. "For steelhead, where I come from," she said. Tough and tightlipped, Jill didn't let much out unless she'd had a few, or the subject was fishing. Her mother and sisters were back in some factory town on Lake Superior. She talked about fishing with them for fish I'd never heard of, walleye and smelt. She told tales about spearfishing at night and high stakes derbies on the Lake. But her tone was humble when the subject was fly fishing. We soon realized we shared more than a bunkroom.

We became partners in our desperation to get out, and partners in crime, shoving whole salmon from the line down our overalls to smoke in a plywood smoker we built behind the trailers. We stole a vise from the shop for late-night fly tying, by flashlight to avoid the curses and hurled boots of exhausted workers asleep in the same room.

We were determined to fish one way or another. Their way, for the challenge and the money. Our way for the sheer love of it.

Out on the dock now, I'm closer to catching fish, closer to the boats, the skippers and crews. Closer to word of an opening, a job as a deckhand, catching fish.

When I first arrived here in flat, brown Bristol Bay, I thought I had a job lined up, friend of a friend kind of thing. I found the guy in a dimly lit boathouse hanging nets. He looked up at me sourly and shrugged, "A mistake," he said, pointing with his elbow to a big man behind him nimbly mending. "He's my crew."

I was crushed, but couldn't let it show, not even to myself. Paralyzed, I turned and slowly walked out. When you get cut, it happens so fast. It hurts, and then it's over. It'll hurt some more if you let yourself think about it. If you don't, the healing starts. No reason to hire me, I told myself, I was green and female. Bad luck on any boat.

Broke, I spent the next two days looking for another boat, offering to work for half a crew share. Still broke, I set my jaw and climbed the hill to the only job in town with nothing to do with fishing. For a week I dug sewer lines in the permafrost with a pick. I silently swore I'd be fishing soon, but my hands were wrecked with blisters. The season opened and I was hired instead down at the processing plant.

Since then I've had a few chances at fishing. I would get an offer and grab my duffle without thought. I would jump on and work my heart out, hauling in the drift nets and picking fish, collapsing, exhausted and elated, between sets. But it never lasted. The skipper was either a drunk, a dealer or a fool. He wanted someone to hit, or hit on, not a deckhand. I would jump off after a few days, sometimes a few hours, to a tender or another boat. I waited all night once, crouched in the darkness, for the tide to come in so I could reach the ladder to the dock above.

It takes a while, I know, to find a good boat with a good skipper. In the meantime, I'm kicking, sorting, sliming, counting, loading, everything, but catching fish.

Gurry

⌒

"We *are* fish," Jill says flatly one night after a few vodkas in the wheelhouse of a tender we just off-loaded.

She picks at the scales in her hair. "We're turning into fish," she says as she peels a few more scales off her arm. I nod and remember yesterday. After nine hours of unloading, a wink, the promise of a cold beer and a crew share had me running as fast as I could in waders, into the locker room, peeling off my gear and layers of sweatshirts. Head under the faucet, scrubbing furiously to get the gurry and scales off my face and neck. Buttoning up my shirt, I grab my coat and stuff my hair under my hat. No time to get anything else. I race back through the freezers and the slime line, back out to the dock and stop cold. No radar sticking up, no lines, no boat. It's dawn again already. The boat is heading out against the tide. I turn away and walk slowly up the mud road to the trailers, insides and shoulders aching.

For weeks, more and more fish keep coming. This is the run, the biggest ever they say. We play our part. We off-load it, sort it, slime it, freeze it and load it back on to tenders and back out to sea to the huge Japanese tramper ships hovering on the horizon.

We sleep a few hours at a time. The days no longer make sense. The overtime adds up. Jill decides one day that, the way she sees it, she must have enough hours now to buy a boat, permit and gear so we can fish next season. The hours go by faster as we try out names for our dream gillnetter.

The boats keep coming in. The totes filled with fish are stacked eight high, all over the dock. We move hundreds of thousands of pounds of fish all day, all night. Fish always coming in. More and more fish. It never slows.

Then one morning it stops. A foreman with a creased brow and low voice says there's a closing. They've shut down fishing. Alaska Fish and Game has ordered twenty-four hours for better escapement. Twenty-four hours to let the salmon up the river with no nets to block their biological pull. Twenty-four hours to guarantee the runs in the years ahead will be just as strong.

For us, it's twenty-four hours without fish. Twenty-four hours of beer, shots and pool. A twenty-four hour shower. Twenty-four hours to look for a real job on a boat catching fish. Twenty-four hours to catch fish. That's it. Without words, we gather our rain gear and waders and head to the trailers.

Under our bunks Jill and I have stashed our rods wrapped in towels and T-shirts, and our flies tied with numb, aching fingers. We will fish, really fish, fly fish, for the next twenty-four hours.

We head down the hill and up the dirt road that winds thirty miles with the Wood River up to the lakes. We catch a ride on the back of a truck loaded with nets. The driver is a commercial fisherman, soon to be a sport fisherman. He offers no explanation and neither do we.

We bump on for an hour until we reach the first lake, Aleknagik. We hop off the moving truck. He's going farther. The sound of grinding gears fades and it's quiet.

There are trees here, mountains in the distance, and fish . . . we know it. We stand alone before a deep and silent lake. We are far away from the slime line, the forklifts and the "prove it to me" stares. We are here for our own fish, not to keep, just to catch.

Jill is already into her waders and in the water. But there's no rush, no time clock, no foreman here. It smells of pine and dust.

Everything is still, except the rings on the surface of the water. It's just us and the fish.

For hours we fish without words, nodding at each other's catch as it's eased back into the welcoming water. Hour after hour we catch and release, grayling, arctic char, Dolly Varden, fish with fins and tails intact, eyes and colors bright. These fish are unrelated somehow to the brown, mutilated salmon we've processed by the ton, hour by hour, for months on end. Shimmering and muscled, they are the souls of the lifeless fish we've mucked from the dark, rusted holds of tenders. These are our fish, momentarily.

In the long light of the Alaska dusk, I cast with a sore and swollen arm. Stubborn tears mix with gurry on my sleeve.

JESSICA MAXWELL

Twelve Flew Into the Cuckoo's Nest

They were supposed to be seven feet long and weigh two hundred pounds. They were supposed to be the biggest salmon in the world and nobody had ever fished them but us . . . so where the hell were they?

IRST OF ALL, you have to belong to the Fishermen's Order of Obsessed Lunatics or you would never do this to yourself. Only a F.O.O.L. would fly fourteen hours across the Pacific on a falling-apart plane with three hundred Chinese people who never turn off their reading lights, ride thirty-seven hours across the Gobi Desert in a sandstorm on a train that never stops doing The Jerk, and drive twelve hours across the steppes of Outer Mongolia in a 1963 Soviet bus without shocks . . . just to catch a damn fish.

Like the other eleven fishing fools in our party, I was there to break the world's record for a salmon taken on a fly. Since Mongolian taimen salmon supposedly weigh up to two hundred pounds, they definitely rate as the biggest on earth, the gonzo gift of the last Last Frontier.

The proper name of the big boys we were after was originally a Carmen Miranda dance tune called "Hucho hucho taimen," "hucho" rhyming with "mucho" and "taimen" rhyming with "amen" as in, "It's going to take mucho amen to catch these suckers." They are native to Mongolia, China and Siberia, though Russian taimen have damn near been fished out. Their Mongolian brethren, on the other hand, have for the last ten thousand years swum free in great thawunking numbers because, as our American outfitter had gleefully informed us, "Mongolians don't fish," a fact that swiftly engendered Mongolian Mystery #1: Just what *were* those deeply rutted paths leading to every good fishing hole?

Scientifically, the genus *Hucho* is part of the salmonoid family, making *Hucho hucho* taimen officially a salmon. But I had my doubts. I come from serious salmon country, the American Northwest, where our platinum-flanked warriors leave the rivers of their birth as mere fingerlings, then spend four, sometimes six years cruising around the North Pacific, dodging killer whales and mile-long ghost nets until their bio-alarms set them on a crash course for home. Nothing, but NOTHING, fights like a Pacific king salmon hooked en route to the spawn, especially on light tackle. I have, for instance, personally witnessed a forty-nine-pound king salmon do red and silver cartwheels until it vanished down the cold back of the Kenai River, and I have had my rowboat towed half a mile up the Inside Passage by a twenty-eight-pounder that inspired a new T-shirt slogan: "Spawn 'Til You Die . . . or Die Trying."

But these local Hucho hucho guys sounded like loiterers at best. The rivers they inhabit all drain into Siberia's big, flat Lake Baikal, not some great wild sea. Mongolian salmon make no distinguished journeys. They don't tick like an erotic time bomb, and they don't ride into town, hides ablazing, on the amber hem of every autumn. In short, they're frauds. Armchair adventurers who'd rather sink than swim and simply hang out in their respective rivers like Jabba the Hutt, going nowhere, taking no chances and getting as big as boats, their one redeeming and embarassingly magnetic sporting quality. Unfortunately, it was late June and the rivers of northern Mongolia were too big and dirty to fish.

So there we were, the two scientists in the party and I, alarmingly close to the Siberian border, groin-deep in the swollen Hongoi River, examining the squirming contents of the gill net the guides had set hours earlier, while a gray cashmere sweater of a sky unraveled above our heads. At the moment, it was the only kind of fishing you could do.

Biologists Frank Haw of Washington state, and Ed Brothers from New York, were just as determined as everyone else to set a new record for the world's largest salmon, which, at the moment, was held by a ninety-seven-pound king taken off Alaska's Kenai Peninsula. Stellar fly fishermen both, they were also hard set on breaking the world's salmon-on-a-fly record. But, being scientists, they were just as determined to discover new species of fish. Mongolia, apparently, has one of the most underexplored fish fauna on earth, and it was still possible to ferret out some uncharted guppy there and maybe even name zee leetle steenker after one's former girlfriend, as a pal of Brothers' had done in Belize. On the off-chance of this minor scientific miracle, Dr. Brothers had lugged two five-gallon tubs of formaldehyde six thousand miles across two continents and four countries, much to the annoyance of Chinese and Mongolian customs officers, who kept accusing him of trying to smuggle in American soy sauce.

Our fish camp, what there was of it, bustled with inactivity on the bank above us. Rogue Atlanta attorney George Polatty, Jr., tried in vain to plug the leaks in his Polish pup tent while Seattle-based flight attendant Kay Kolt talked Norwegian physician Haakon "Hawk" Ragde into switching tents with her because a handsome Mongolian fishing guide named Bayara had just promised to "wisit her tonight." Wyoming construction mogul Park Gail and our perma-saturated tour leader, Tom Knight, chased off the lobotomizing effects of last night's Ghengis Khan Vodka with Chinese beer, and twenty-nine-year-old Oregon fly-fishing TV-show host Guido Rahr, sat outside the lone cooking yurt tying flies. Stuart Burnett, a Hong Kong hotel executive, Granger Avery, a country doc from British Columbia and Eric Peterson, another B.C.'er and a co-owner of a fishing resort, were inside huddling around the cookstove beneath brightly painted ceiling spokes strung with several racks of rapidly aging mutton. The only audible voice was George Polatty's, who kept muttering: "Comm'nist bullshit."

Our fishing guides—Mongolians all—sat around their campfire some five yards from the yurt. Russian cigarettes fished for oxygen from the sides of their Mongolian mouths as they sharpened the many hooks protruding from fishing lures made out of some sort of black Third World foam rubber—strange, porous obelisks meant to imitate a swimming Mongolian mouse. Once in a while, a hand would reach into a bag of little Mongolian bakery cakes with indecipherable symbols branded onto their tops, and every so often a cigarette ash would crash and burn on a knee and no one noticed.

This was the first day at fish camp. This was what we woke up to after a sleepless night spent between the one-inch Mongolian cotton mattresses that separated us from the ancient Mongolian earth, and the half-inch Mongolian horse blankets that weren't much help against the effects of subfreezing temperatures on flesh accustomed to central heating or, at least, goose down. This was Mongolia in June. Nothing to write home about, but then you'd get there three months before your letter would anyhow.

The night before had been better—real hotel beds in Ulan Bator, Mongolia's bleak capital city. The train from Beijing had finally deposited us there after three days of Sino-Soviet weirdness, including a seven-hour Saturday night layover at the border, where we changed wheels to accommodate Mongolia's wider-gauge tracks. A few fishermen escaped to the border bar, where Russian soldiers threw back shots of Mongolian vodka while neon signs flashed in time to Eastern-bloc rock. The rest of us got locked in our sleeping car and sweated through that clanking, brutal surgery in the dark while "The Waltz of the Blue Danube" gargled out of the train station loud speaker. From somewhere not too far away, human screams ruptured the black spleen of the night. Then there was gunshot. "Ah don't know if they were shootin' at a rabbit or us," George Polatty said, "but the screamin' sure stopped. Comm'nist bullshit."

As with other Soviet satellite countries at that time, the current Mongolian zeitgeist carried distinct anti-Russian sentiments as the country readied for its first free elections in seventy years. We had been warned to keep a low profile lest we be mistaken for Russians and get the hell beaten out of us. Not exactly the most propitious time for a certain well-oiled American angler to pump the many-medaled shoulder of a very large Mongolian customs officer and slur in no uncertain terms that we were "gonna catch the biggest f—in' fish in the world." Fortunately, the man refrained from reducing the offending fisherman to goat manure.

We spent the rest of the night crossing the Gobi Desert while its insidious grit stormed the failing shell of that old railroad mollusk, scouring our eyes and lungs raw, making miniature sand dunes against our windows and turning our hair to Brill-O. Sleep being a pipe dream, one found oneself falling into Fellini-esque conversations with, say, a Hungarian Professor named Dr. Lajosgooz who insisted that "Mongolians don't want to start agriculture because they don't want to hurt Mother Earth." Morning came on cool and bright, a mother-of-pearl sky edged in flat lace clouds. Antelope and wild camel loped across the taupe-colored earth for miles beyond our windows. "Looks just like Madison Basin in Montana," Frank Haw said. An attendant served us tea. In the dining car, the menu announced that "Food is Welcome" and we breakfasted on "Hot Animal Food," including "Borscht Moscow," steamed meat dumplings called "buuz," both kefir and "soured cream," and "Fried eggs with fresh spring onions."

The air in Ulan Bator was charged and sharp. Built on the lap of the steppes, wild continental zephyrs play the capital's dreary collection of Soviet-designed blocks like dull chimes. The city feels huddled and lost, and urbanization remains an impossible command barked into the Mongolian wind.

The hotel air, like everything else, was laminated with mutton fat and the plumbing sounded like horns honking and donkeys. In the morning a maid walked right into my room and slammed the window shut, while a six-point bull elk trotted between the buses on the street below.

That time of year the winds bring the rains, and the great Mongolian plains bloom and soften...then turn to mud, the bottom-line of our all-day bus ride to fish camp—a chiropractor's horror movie, with very strange subtitles which Ed Brothers interpreted at regular intervals as "time to turn the other cheek." But our discomfort dissolved wholly at the feet of a vision burned once and forever into our burdened North American image banks: a lone herdsman. In a purple robe with a gold sash, a black bowler hat and tall black boots. Holding aloft a long polished tree branch lance with a rope loop at its front end. Standing up in his stirrups and posting silently across Mongolia's extravagant grasslands.

Like the sites of all classic Western films, Mongolia is high plateau country. And our fish camp, when we finally got there, was slugged up in its northern forest on the green, green décolletage of a very pretty river valley. Birch and willow fluoresced chartreuse and new against the muddied ruin of the water. Our tents lay in the tender grasses above them. And the hills were alive with tamarack, not to mention wolves, wolverines, wild boar, Roe deer, elk, Siberian moose, pit vipers—which really prefer tender grasses—possibly snow leopard, and most certainly Asian brown bear, which were just waking up and thinking about going over the mountain to see what they could see.

On fishing trips, you can count on the natural beauty to nurture you when conditions can't. Or, as Kay Kolt put it: "I always give myself three days to catch a fish: one for weather, one to get to know the water, and one for luck." My own fishing record is substantially less productive—about once a month I get lucky. The only explanation I've ever come up with is hormones: if I'm ovulating I'll catch every fish in the river. Unfortunately, this trip was going to miss my "O-Zone" by a week.

In barely mixed company, discussion topics naturally detour around any mention of feminine cycles. And with so many guy scientists in the group, questions tended to veer toward the academic, such as: how can a closed river system support such lunkers?

"Horses," Dr. Brothers replied, staring hopefully at the Mongolian minnows toodling around in his bucket.

We'd all seen the stories: "PEKING (UPI)—Thousands of Chinese tourists have visited a remote lake in western China to glimpse a horse-eating water monster...." And, "At least 50 horses and a dozen men have been eaten alive by a 35-foot fish that swallows its victims whole, the New China News Agency reports." These clips, supplied, it turned out, by Brothers himself, were part of the Mongolia hype distributed to all us eager anglers by Kleinburger Worldwide Travel, the Seattle-based travel agency that had arranged our trip.

For twenty years, the agency has taken big-game hunters into this boreal wilderness in pursuit of Mongolia's macro-rack elk. With the civilized world finally waking up to the deep creepiness of trophy hunting, the agency decided to add fishing to its repertoire. When I heard about this once-in-a-lifetime chance to be part of the First Western Mongolian Salmon Fishing Expedition, I suffered a serious glee attack. Salmon are my totem. My original call of the wild. They are role models for three of the traits I value most: tenacity, courage and passion. I even met my husband in an Alaskan salmon smokery—our wedding rings are twin gold salmon joined at the tail. The only way I'd be kept from fishing Mongolia in person was if they built a dam between my house and the airport.

When I finally arrived I was hypnotized. Mongolia is ravishing, like the Great Plains before contact, an endless wind-washed grassland slung between forested edges and mountains so old and wind-worn you felt like scampering up one just to get a God's-eye view of the place.

"Damn if it doesn't look like western Montana," Frank Haw said again, nodding at the handsome woodlands around us.

"Montana with cuckoo clocks," Brothers grumbled.

Nine times in the last seven minutes, we had been obliged to suffer what Austrians must endure only once an hour—the demented call of the cuckoo, which surely would be Mongolia's state bird, if the place were a state.

Mongolia was then, in fact, a Communist republic—the Mongolian People's Republic—and had been since 1924. It's big...and empty—about four times the size of Montana, slightly larger than Alaska, with the population of Oregon. Actually, most Mongols have migrated to Chinese territory, having been run off by the Communists, the cuckoo birds, the weather (minus fifty-four degrees one winter), and names that look like the bottom line of an eye-chart. Agbaanjantsangiyn Jamsranjab, for instance, Mongolia's then Minister of Public Security, and Choyjiljabyn Tserennadmid, its then Minister of Health, and its former president, Punsalmaagiin Ochirbat.

The Mongols who stayed home are super-Mongolians. Bored silly with Soviet dweebiness, they had, not long before our visit, called for a cultural renaissance, bringing back Ghengis Khan, the Mongolian alphabet and the golden *soyombo*—the Mongolian national emblem consisting of a flame, the sun, the moon, two triangles, four rectangles and, Mongolian Mystery #2: Two FISH! All of which explains why our interpreter, mercifully named Basa, looked like a Nepalese rabbi. Like the lone herdsman, he walked around camp in a brown robe sashed with gold—the traditional Mongolian dress code, give or take color choice.

Mongolia is still ninety percent grasslands, and half of its 2.1 million people are still nomadic, running their twenty-five million horses, goats, camels and sheep over the wide open steppes. They have Eskimo good looks—brown skin, Asian eyes, cheekbones like hard-boiled eggs—and a rumored national proclivity for promiscuity that has given Mongolia the nickname "Sweden of the south."

This fact titillated our boys enough to instantly inspire a trip motto: "Swe-den! Swe-den!" . . . until our own Dr. Ragde, a prostate specialist, broke the news that Mongolia hosts a virtual smorgasbord of venereal diseases, many of which are untreatable and lethal. Thus did our fisherman's war-cry revert to the original: "Cuckoo. Cuckoo."

The second morning flowered above us like the wild iris that bloom all over northern Outer Mongolia in June. The sky looked like Liz Taylor's eyes, and the river looked like the rest of her. Though, still out of shape, its big belly had gone down an inch or so, and fishing parties were organized. That day I fished with Polatty, Peterson, Rahr, Burnett and Avery.

After a breakfast of bread, butter, Rumanian cherry jam, instant coffee glazed with a film of mutton fat, and cubed Mongolian mutton, and after Hawk Ragde led a successful campaign to trade six bottles of vodka and two cases of beer for at least one sleeping yurt, we headed out. We had been promised sleeping yurts with wood floors. We had also been promised a "Soviet-built four-wheel-drive vehicle with driver and an English-speaking interpreter for each two clients." What we had was Pup Tents From Hell, a jeep, a flat-bed truck . . . and Basa. And an assortment of local guides who could only say "Elvees Presleey" except for Bayara, that Mongolian Romeo, who clearly picked up his English from Prince albums. We all piled into the truck and took off downriver.

Being a girl in a seriously macho country has its advantages—I got to sit in the cabin with the driver, Tim-ul, and look at the "Welcome to Mongolia" stickers on the dash. Each one featured a different animal: elk, deer, big horn sheep, snow leopard, moose, a drooling brown bear. Tim-ul pointed to the wolf sticker and made a gunning engine noise: "Chun! Chun!" Then he did a git-along-little-doggies motion with his hands and said, "Yo-*ho!* Yo-*ho!*," Mongolian for "go," burying the "o" sound like those pit-of-the-stomach German words that mean "he has hair on his teeth." Mostly, though, Mongolian sounds like a cross between Arabic and Hawaiian, a kind of ancient gut music spoken by a people who have the wind of the steppes in their souls.

Our group was let off last. We did not get Basa. We got "Fish Master," whose real name sounded like "Tigshee," which certain incorrigible members of the group secretly mistook for a certain barnyard by-product.

Fish Master had made it clear to Basa that we Westerners had already made three critical mistakes: "too much luggage, too thin fishing line and too small hooks." Mongolians fish to catch fish. They do not understand the sport of trying to take a big one on the lightest line possible. They think that's cuckoo.

Fish Master also regarded our super flies with disgust. Given taimen's carnivorous reputation, we had been busy tying huge Mariboo Muddlers with spun deer-hair heads, white and black mariboo wings, and silver-and-gold tinseled bodies. Gaudy, nine-inch Las Vegas monsters that would give any American trout heart failure. We were also well stocked with giant deer-hair mice called Lefty's Deceivers. And Guido had tied some sinewy macro-streamers with colored synthetic hair that looked like Magic Pony roadkills.

Given our sorry lure selection, Fish Master felt it necessary to demonstrate the overriding wisdom of the Swimming Mongolian Mouse. Having led us swiftly across difficult terrain riffled with dirt mounds to which he pointed and made wild boar snorts, we finally broke through a stand of birch and found ourselves on an elbow of sandy beach. In a stunning breach of American fishing-guide etiquette, Fish Master cast first. Upstream, no less. He drew his floating mouse across the old Hongoi River and got nothing. He cast again and got a substantial strike. "Tuul," he said coolly, which is Mongolian for taimen, and reeled in with strange, subtle jerks. The fish surfaced sluggishly, flashing salmon-colored fins. It had no fight in it and an ugly green triangular head. Fish Master beached it proudly. It weighed fourteen pounds.

Fish Master then decided to examine my tackle, which, at the moment, was one of the smart little deer-hair mice Guido and I had tied out of caribou fur lifted from an old rug in the cooking yurt. We had set up a vise right there, tied on a little leather mousey tail, then held the caribou in small bundles and spun it around the shank of the hook until the ends flared out. We packed it up the head of the hook, tied on two little leather ears, then spun more caribou hair behind the hook's eye to make a little varmint head. Finally we gave the thing a haircut, shaping it lovingly into a damn respectable facsimile of a mouse.

Fish Master pronounced it useless, gave it the equivalent of a Mongolian raspberry, and looted Polatty's tackle box until he found a simple brass French lure called a Mepps #5. He tied it to

my line with the exasperated motions of a parent wiping chocolate off the face of a child in church. Against my deepest philo-
sophical values I tried the thing and instantly got a small taimen,
which my conscience bade me lose in the shallows.

When Fish Master stopped pestering me, I secretly switched
back to my little rug-rat fly and cast fruitlessly but happily away
into the Montana light of a Mongolian afternoon.

All in all, our group took a couple of graylings and a good-
sized lenok, which is an unremarkable fish except for being the
oldest species of trout in the world, and that was about it for the
rest of the day.

The new sleeping yurt was up by the time we got back to camp.
Polatty, Brothers, Avery, Burnett, Ragde and Kolt abandoned
their pup tents for a space on its tender grassy floor. We were
further heartened by the announcement that dinner duties that
night would be taken over by Eric Peterson, who had responded
to pretrip warnings of Mongolia's subgustatory cuisine by lug-
ging in two jumbo coolers stocked with Dijon, marmalade,
wasabe, jerkins, whole pepper corns and a grinder, rosemary,
thyme, oregano, curry powder, Korean kim chee, Swiss soup
mix, Japanese ramen, an arsenal of English biscuits, Italian olive
oil, French pate, Norwegian sardines, smoked oysters, anchovy
paste, Jarlsberg cheese, American peanut butter, a case of fine
wine, fresh produce from Beijing and many jars of Russian caviar
plucked from Ulan Bator's black market. Chinese and Mongolian
customs officers naturally assumed he was neck-deep in some international gourmet import scam with Ed Brothers.

Peterson opted to cook up Fish Master's taimen which Brothers offered to fillet. He was really after the otoliths, tiny, leaf-

shaped ear stones lodged deep in a fish's head. Brothers is one of the world's experts at aging fish by reading their ear stones, but first he has to suck the gunk off them with his mouth. While people held their stomachs and pretended to look at the scenery, Slime-Breath Brothers finally announced that Fish Master's taimen was around ten years old. Its flesh was firm and creamy white and looked—and, once cooked, tasted—a lot like trout. While the welcomed perfumes of Chinese garlic and lemon rode the air around the cooking yurt, Dr. Brothers also reported that his net had taken yet another species.

"The family common name is loach," he said, displaying an uneventful-looking fish. Then he told us that a tropical cousin of the one he caught gets hyperactive when low pressure fronts move in, and is, therefore, called the "weather fish." "There's also an air-breathing loach whose gut tissue stores oxygen," Brothers added. "When the barometric pressure changes, it flips over and flatulates out its air. We call those the 'farting weather fish.'" As people backed away from Brothers and his fish bucket, Fish Master told Basa to tell us that we would go fishing that night.

"After dinner?" Dr. Ragde asked, imagining a good evening bite.

"No, at midnight," Basa translated.

Cuckoo. Cuckoo.

Fishing on a moonless midnight in Outer Mongolia with non-English-speaking guides who had Ghengis Khan Vodka for supper takes guts. More than I had, but then I'd learned that equation in high school: Boys + Alcohol + Fast Cars = Health Hazard 101. Nonetheless, Eric Peterson went. So did Polatty,

Avery, Burnett, Rahr and Brothers, who fishes for brown trout late June nights in the upper Delaware River back home in Ithaca and somehow missed the Alcohol + Fast Cars part. He had even tied his own version of the Swimming Mongolian Mouse for the event—a trimmed-spun-elk hair rodent with a chamois tail, which he christened the "Lemming Meringue Fly."

They took the jeep and the truck, the drivers of which played chicken in the dark the whole way. And in case a bear showed up, the fishing guides also took guns, one of which was on the floor of the truck cabin pointed at Eric Peterson's head.

Guido didn't like the idea of night fishing with guns. "It's too dark to see anything," he said. "If you hit a bear, you'd probably just wound it."

Rahr, Basa and one of the drivers hiked over to a wide, deep pool in the Sharlon River, a tributary, like the Hongoi, of the Uro River, which began at their confluence just downstream from our fish camp. Stars glittered through the treetops like animal eyes, and the river looked like eels. Rahr waded up to his waist and cast into the darkness trying not to remember the UPI stories about horse-eating fish. "If the big ones do come out at night," he thought, "I'm hamburger."

There was a commotion upstream. The driver had just lost a fish on single forty-pound test line. The leader was double strand forty-pound test, and he had been fishing a Mongolian mouse the size of a rat with three sets of hooks. The fish broke off two inches above the lure. Both strands of the leader were badly frayed. The fish had swallowed the mouse whole.

So the Hucho honchos *were* there. And even though in seventeen years of fishing Fish Master had produced only an eighty-pound taimen, Rahr shifted into high gear. He dead-drifted the riffles. He worked the pools. He dragged the tailouts. Fishing blind, he cast and cast again into the black Mongolian night. He didn't catch a thing. But he couldn't help hoping there was a big one out there somewhere, waiting for Guido.

George Polatty came closer the following day, our third day at fish camp and second day of fishing. Avoiding yet another bread and mutton breakfast, he and Park Gail left camp early to fish the Sharlon. After catching one too many lenok, Polatty switched to a #5 Mepps spinner and got a serious strike. It was a taimen. It jumped clean out of the water three times, dove straight down and jumped again. It didn't run. They never do. Finally it rolled over on the line and broke off. Polatty says it was six feet long and weighed a good eighty pounds. Gail agrees.

Meanwhile, Guido and I had about drowned our deer-hair mice and showgirl streamer patterns. And we had precious little to show for it. By dinnertime, none of us had landed the kind of newsmaker jumbo salmon we had come for. All we had was a mess of little lenok and grayling. Morale was knee-high to a pit viper, and we were all ready to request cuckoo bird hors d'oeuvres. Instead we were treated to a local specialty—smoked lenok, which our fishing guides cooked whole over their camp-fire. It was fabulous, a miracle of smoky tenderness, and it swiftly generated Mongolian Mystery #3: Just how does a popu-lace that doesn't fish know how to make bar mitzvah-quality lox?

Around noon the next day a Soviet helicopter landed in the field in front of our camp. A clutch of Mongolians in 1957 western clothes deplaned and walked toward the cooking yurt. Basa addressed them, then explained they were from the Ministry of the Protection of Nature. Delighted—and relieved—we requested an audience. After some twenty minutes, we were invited inside. The men were seated cross-legged on the floor or lounging around on the rugs, Mongolian style. I asked about the future of western fishing expeditions there. Their leader, a Mr. Badam, said "Western fishermen are welcome" and he "wishes us success." Then we were dismissed. The officials stayed in the cooking yurt for several hours. They had come, it was clear, for lunch. George Polatty shook his head, "Comm'nist bullshit."

By mid-afternoon it was 75 degrees and the river looked very good. Guido Rahr and I walked upstream to the Mother of All Bridges and cast a few under it, still overworking our deer mice to the point of exhaustion. Guido was more frustrated than I was. Maybe it was the wrong time of the month, but my killer instinct had curled up in the sun with a good book. Mongolia or no, the place felt like home, abloom with all the appointments that make fishing rivers so grand—the dry flutter of tree leaves, the blue eye of the sky, a soothing breeze, real air, the Champagne chill of the water and its uncorked musical gargle.

Many anglers confess to the fact that before long they expect to be happy just standing around in nature with nothing much to do, that catching a fish even now is secondary to fishing and may become utterly unnecessary. I, myself, was hovering on the cusp of such passive contentment when Brothers walked by. He'd been fishing the Sharlan and told us about a new pool he'd found. "I was trailing an ugly rabbit-hair Dahlberg Diver there," he reported, "and on my second cast this huge green head came up behind the fly—must have been a good six or seven inches between the eyes. It opened its mouth, then just closed it again and slowly sank back down." And that was it for The Pacifist

Within. Without a word Guido and I packed up and headed for Ed's Pool.

We hiked upriver through iris and yellow poppies and banks of what looked to be wild strawberry heavy with white blossoms. The *soyombo* sun blazed above, turning the river to chrome, and you couldn't help wondering why Mongolia didn't look less like the foothills of the American Rockies and more like Pluto.

Ed's Pool was a beautiful thing. Quiet, like jade slag trimmed in a cowl of sandy beach. Granite cliffs rose heavenward on the other side, crowned with stands of birch. It was as if we were fishing a subterranean stream in the basement of the forest, and the strangesse it produced somehow made us come to our senses. The big deer-hair flies just weren't working. It was time for a change.

"Let's fish for these guys the way we know how," Guido suggested while I was already digging around for some little black nymphs.

We should have thought of this before. Even Ed had reported that the fish in this pool took one look at his big gawd-awful frog patterns and just turned around.

I cast into the long run below the pool and let my fly swing at the end of the drift. Bam! A lenok hit within seconds. It fought like a somewhat freaked-out champ, albeit one shocked by what surely must have been its first time to be hoisted through the water by its lip. When I released it the poor thing almost spontaneously combusted with relief.

Guido got one next, and then another; I landed a fourth. Then Guido remembered that he had some lead-eyed sculpin in his fly box left over from a fishing trip to the Yellow Breeches River near Harrisburg, Pennsylvania. They had black mariboo tails, black chenille bodies and black deer-hair heads studded with little black sticking-out lead eyes that made them sink, a classic fly pattern developed for the region's brown trout. Limestone stream brownies, they call them, native to the Yellow Breeches as well as Spring Creek and Pennsylvania Creek—famous trout streams all, where some of the first American fly fishing began more than a hundred years ago. Old sculpin patterns like those seemed an appropriate offering to the ancient waters of Mongolia where they would surely imitate one of Ed Brothers' little black loaches swimming hard.

Guido cast first. Instantly, a fish hit—a big lenok. He released it and cast again. His cream-colored line drew pale snakes in the air. "I feel lucky," he said. The announcement activated my finest fishing manners. I stayed off the water.

Guido's lead-eyed sculpin sailed into the deepest corner of the pool, and like the counterweight of a theater drape, when it landed and sank, the curtain rose. From somewhere offstage, the Mongolian Weather Gods blew a sudden strong wind upriver, and the birch leaves rattled overhead like money. Rolling thunder exploded in the aisle of sky above us and the songbirds went nuts, shrieking alarms and dive-bombing my hair. The air smelled possessed, full of ozone and ions, and the clouds kept doubling over and then standing up taller than before. Finally, like a play within a play, Guido Rahr got a major fish on.

"This is it," he said. "I'm going for a world record."

In a swirl of peach tail fin, the fish turned and Guido turned with it, his right arm flung out sideways like Nureyev. The fish took a dive, and Guido let it run, his reel spinning in the palm of his hand. The taimen turned again, and again Guido stepped gracefully aside, locked into the holy communion between fisherman and fish, the water ballet that renders angling angelic, elevating the sport beyond the usual life and death struggle. When the rain came twenty minutes later, Guido beached his fish, an eleven-pound beautiful-ugly Mongolian *Hucho hucho* taimen, the king of the wild frontier.

Then it was my turn. I cast far, letting the heavy eyes of the sculpin sink to the sandy bottom and drift left. The rain-stippled surface of the river blurred my water vision, and I used my fly like physical sonar, letting it bounce the contours of the river bottom back across my index finger in jolts and hops.

Guido saw it first, surfacing in an ungodly display of triangular terribleness. Flat green head, sick orange skin, Ed's Monster Taimen. It was, there is no doubt, my one and only chance to land the world's biggest—and ugliest—salmon on a fly, however my instincts had other ideas. Let's just say that my body reacted to that rising mass of icky ichthyology the same way it did when my computer screen filled with pulsing green "V's" and announced "Internal Stack Failure. Exit Now!" I ran screaming out of the room . . . or, in this case, the river. I'd be damned if I was going to set a world record with a fish that looked so much like Quasimodo in a mermaid suit that I was afraid to be in the water with it.

The storm delivered many Mongolian salmon that day. Granger Avery took a fourteen-pounder as long as his arm. So did Frank Haw, on eight-pound test. George Polatty landed a five-pound taimen on four-pound test. "I reckon I got a world record with this one," he reckoned. He reckoned right. No one from the West had ever fished taimen before; the International Game Fish Association had no categories for them. You could catch a quarter-pound taimen with a stick and set a world record. We were competing only against ourselves.

Kay Kolt was right. It had taken three days to nail these bo-zos, lightweights that they were. This conditional victory is the only explanation for the ensuing Night of Mongolian Madness. After supper, everyone just piled into the sleeping yurt and pounded down several bottles of Genghis Khan. At 3:00 A.M., the yurt still glowed like a fallen star beneath the Mongolian night, and if you listened closely, between the animal cries and the call of the cuckoo you could make out the party's theme song: "Tai-ai-ai-men is on my line, yes it is!"

By noon the next day ninety percent of the anglers were still sleeping it off. With the noble exception of Ed Brothers, who, de-spite a ripping case of vodka fog, went fishing and finally got his record-setting taimen, a ten-pounder on eight-pound test. He would have used four, but that's what Rahr had taken his fish on, so Brothers switched to eight to ensure world records for both of them.

We would submit four: Polatty's and Haw's in the Freshwa-ter Line classes, Brothers' and Rahr's in the Fly Rod catagory. And, in the end, Haw's eight-pound line would test out at twelve, Polatty's four-pound line would test out at eight, and so would Rahr's, knocking Brothers' slightly lighter fish caught on certi-fied eight-pound line out of the world record book forever.

Our last day at fish camp broke like a raw egg, the yolk of the sun sliding down the backside of a very misty morning. Everyone was busy packing when Ed Brothers and George Polatty discov-ered the pit viper between their bedrolls. It was a young one, but it definitely had a pit, a heat-seeking hole beside one nostril, which explains what it was doing in the sleeping yurt.

Polatty had picked it up to examine it, holding it behind its head, when one of the Mongolians came racing down the river bank screaming "Bear!" It was definitely time to go home.

In a suite at the Hotel Ulan Bator that night, a special meeting was held. Frank Haw, Ed Brothers, Guido Rahr, Tom Knight and I wanted a chance to discuss Mongolian fish conservation with Basa and his boss, Mr. Bator, the president of Zhuulchin, Mongolia's official travel agency, which arranges all trips.

We knew Mongolia was ripe for the late twentieth century, full of copper, gold, silver, coal and, unfortunately, oil, which both American and British industrialists can't wait to get their hands on. We knew that Japan had already entered into a joint venture with Mongolia to manufacture steel, cashmere and electronics, and JAL Airlines was trying to establish a direct route from Tokyo to Ulan Bator. We knew Mongolia was moving fast toward economic development. But we hoped that in this initial rush to be like the West, we Westerners might offer a word of caution, an educated plea that Mongolians value what Mongolia is and has managed to remain, while the rest of the world plunders itself into a toxic coma.

"Taimen are *precious*," I practically pleaded.

"They really are rare," Brothers confirmed.

"We'll send you a book on the biology of these fish," Haw offered.

"Dis book *wery* useful," Basa replied. "Vee *need* information."

"In my reading I've learned that these fish are getting more and more scarce," Haw went on. "There's no reason not to practice catch-and-release."

"You don't have to kill a fish," our suddenly animated, always besotted leader Tom Knight offered. "You can make a fiberglass replica of it."

"You should know that a number of streams in the United States are catch-and-release only," I said.

"We have catch-and-release streams *and* kill streams," Rahr reminded. "And it's not fair to lock off streams from the locals."

"All along the rivers we saw evidence of local fishing," Knight said.

"Mongolians, they don't listen," Basa replied. "We do have licenses."

"There are legal problems," Mr. Bator admitted. "Inspectors come maybe four times a month."

"You need to develop a plan," Haw said.

"We've found that local nonprofit organizations can be an enormous help," Rahr said.

"Yes," I concurred, sending small conspiratorial eye-daggers to Guido. "They do the work our government *should* be doing."

"Vee might start a fish association party," Basa replied. "I have dis in my head to do."

"How can we call it?" Mr. Bator asked. "The National Foundation of Fish?"

Tom Knight grinned. "Hey, we're in on the ground floor of a fisheries management program, here!"

"You'll want to be careful about damming, too," Haw went on. "Dams stop migration and can wipe out a whole run of fish," Rahr warned.

"Oh, our Green Party is fighting against dis," Basa informed us. "Dey want zero dams planned for beeg rivers."

"THE GREEN PARTY?" Everyone gasped. "In *Mongolia?*"

"Oh, yes," Basa replied. "Vee have dee Green Party and many nature parties. But vee don't have a fish party." He paused for a moment, and then he smiled. "Mongolian fishes are wery lucky, maybe," he said. "Vee are a Buddhist country, and Buddhism says, 'Don't touch snakes and vater animals.' Until I vas fifteen years old, I vas told by my mother, 'Don't touch fishes—dis is evil to do.' Dis is maybe a good ting."

And this maybe meant that Mongolia was in better shape than we thought it was. Maybe, then, we could all go home knowing we could come back in ten years and the Big Green Ones would still be there with the snow leopards and the bears, the wolves and the wild boar and the idiotic cuckoos, despite the fact that Brothers had lobbied hard for year-round open season on them. And maybe in ten years we'd still have to take a bone-busting bus ride to fish camp, and somewhere along the way our hearts would thrill again to the sight of a lone Mongolian cowboy, dressed like Ghengis Khan himself, riding high in his saddle across the generous purple steppes of Outer Mongolia.

LE ANNE SCHREIBER

Midstream

Glenco Mills, N.Y. ◆ *Tuesday, April 16, 1985*

I AM BEGINNING to notice different things now. The softness of Midnight's fur, the pale green of his eyes and how the blackness opens from a vertical slit in his pupil to a full roundness in fright, overwhelming the inquiring green. The pinkness that edges a brook trout's fins, the

Editor's note: This is an excerpt from Le Anne Schreiber's memoir Midstream: The Story of a Mother's Death and a Daughter's Renewal *(Viking, 1990). Soon after Schreiber moved to a house in a rural hamlet in the Hudson River Valley, where she found the ideal trout stream and mastered the art of the cast, she learned that her mother had pancreatic cancer. The journal she kept during the two years of her mother's illlness and death follows Schreiber as she struggles with her loss and finds solace in her new country home.*

signal that something alive is nestled among the stones at the bottom of the stream. The grayish-green of their bodies blends so completely with the color of the stones that until I see the strip of slightly undulating white, I cannot discern the possibility of their sudden, startling flight.

I wonder now what creatures see. When I watch birds feeding through the red grid of my kitchen window, do they see me? They must, because they see Midnight at the pantry door and take off in skittish flight, cardinals first and chickadees last. But do they see my colors? form? movement?

I am struck for the first time by the miracle of perennials—dry, dead sticks putting forth buds or making way for new growth from the old roots. The dried remains of last year's flowers are still on their stalks while new plants spring up between their legs, seeking a share of light and air. In my borrowed garden, I clear away the old growth to make room for the new. But down the road, in Bruno's untended garden, the old stalks remain and new shoots find their way among them anyway. Maybe mine is an American impulse and Bruno, a French vintner's son, knows something I don't.

It has taken me, daughter of a farmer's daughter, forty years to discover these things, and belated as I am, I choose the slow way of learning, just observing what happens each day and guessing at what tomorrow will bring. I have no desire to go to books that might explain these things to me, how flowers grow, how trout make their way through the seasons, natural and legal.

Friday, April 19

I have been listening to fitful rolls of thunder for the past half hour. The sky is dark and the air still, but just when it seems about to storm, the sun bursts through the clouds and it's a sunny spring afternoon again. Just now, the sky turned gray-green and I hear the first faint drops, slow and tentative.

The thunder brought me home from the stream where, again, I fished without catching anything. It makes little difference to me whether I get a bite. I am still learning my rod and reel. Last Friday, I took the old reel apart to learn its secrets, then I put a new reel on the rod and filled it with line, discovering every tangle trial and error can produce. It's a task that requires four hands, and I had to make do with two and a pair of knees.

After several days of casting, I have become comfortable, even intimate with my rod, but I still discover something new about it every day. Yesterday, by accident, I cast farther than I ever had before, and then I realized it was the way I snapped my wrist that produced the effect. Before the cast, I had been whipping my arm slower or faster, in a longer or shorter arc, to control the distance, but now I see it is in the wrist, not the arm and shoulder, that distance is determined.

Discovering this, I realized I had known it all along; it was familiar but forgotten knowledge, something I had read or, more likely, been told by my father in childhood. Now I have learned it in a way I will not forget, on my own wrist.

Today, some instinct told me to pull the rod backward at the end of a cast, and suddenly I had solved the problem of slack that snarled my line when I started to reel it in. Discovering this, I again remembered that I had known it; the motion was one I'd seen my father make hundreds of times, but I never realized it had a purpose. I thought it was one of those poses that belong to men, like standing with hands on hips, head bowed, after exertion. I thought the rod-jerking motion intrinsic to men, not to fishing, just as I once thought the hands-on-hips posture belonged to men, not to deep breathing.

There was a time when certain actions, performed by me, made me feel both exhilarated and confused. Exhilarated because I knew I was trespassing where no girls were allowed, and it was dangerous, exciting. Confused, because it made me wonder if I was a true girl if such actions came unbeckoned to my body. Once, when I was standing, head bowed, hands on hips, after a long run in a touch football game, my college boyfriend said, "I hate to see you standing like that." I became self-conscious, and for the rest of the game tried to avoid that stance, but my body wouldn't cooperate, and then I realized it was because bodies, any bodies, want to do that when they need to catch a deep breath.

Thursday, April 25

Today I bought a "sportsman's tool" at Ames—a pocket-size wrench, pliers, wire cutter in one. I'm using it to cut two of the three hooks off all my lures, so that when I catch an undersized fish, I can return it to the stream undamaged.

Tuesday, an hour before sunset, I went to the part of the stream that runs directly behind the house and waded my way upstream to a stretch of fast-flowing water that has several deep, eddying pools in it. I planned to start fishing above the fast water and work my way downstream, making a few casts into each of the pools.

At the first pool, I hooked a six-inch brook trout. When I tried to release the fish, I saw it had swallowed the lure, two hooks embedded up and down its throat. I tugged the line, and the trout flapped in my hand, rolling its eyes in panic. I put it back in the water, hoping against reason the fish might free itself by thrashing. A minute later, I hauled it back onto the rocks and tried to work the lure free with my hands, but it was clear the only way to remove the lure was by jerking the line so hard it would tear the fish apart.

I put it back in the water again, took it out again. Each time I returned the fish to the stream, it seemed more listless, and its flesh, a glistening greenish-black when first caught, was becoming an eerie, phosphorescent silver. I talked to the fish as if it were Midnight. "Oh, honey, I'm so sorry. It'll be all right. Just let me help." I cursed myself for going fishing without a knife to cut the line. At one point I decided to put the fish out of its misery, but the only way to kill it was by smashing it with a rock, and I couldn't bring myself to do that. Finally I yanked the line between my two hands and it broke, leaving the lure embedded in the trout's throat. I returned him to the stream alive, but I know he can't survive.

Wading back home as the sun set, feeling miserable, depressed and guilty, I vowed never to fish again. But gradually, as the water swirling around my knees turned from gold to lavender and then to dark purple, I began to persuade myself that I could still spend my days in the stream, I could still fish if I did it in some way that guaranteed I would be able to release what I caught. So this morning I tried to remove two of the three hooks from my lures with scissors and a hammer. I tried cutting the hooks off, bending them straight, nothing worked. Finally, I called my father in Minnesota to ask him how to fish without maiming the catch, and he told me about the "sportsman's tool." He suggested I try fly fishing with the rod he left behind on his visit last fall.

As soon as I mentioned I was having problems with three-hook lures, I could tell he understood. His voice became quiet and steady, full of inflectionless concern, as he described the tool and what it could do. He was talking to me the way I had talked to the fish. "It'll be all right, honey. Just do as I say and it'll be all right. . . . "

Sunday, May 5

Last night I dreamt that Mom and I were driving in an open-topped jeep on a country road at night. We were driving through a wooded area on a narrow road that went up and down hills, round curves and over bridges, a road like many of those I drive around here.

In the dream Mom was driving and I kept telling her to be careful, because she didn't seem to see that both shoulders of the road were lined with deer. She was driving fast and I was afraid we would hit one of them. I didn't think we were in danger; my concern was for the deer.

As we approached a small bridge, my attention was fixed on the shadowy forms and red eyes caught in the glare of our head-lights, when all of a sudden, a black bear lunged out of the woods. Before I could scream, he leapt through the car, grabbed Mom's head in his jaws and landed with her in the stream under the bridge.

Terrified and in shock, I stopped the jeep and ran back to the bridge. The bear had the back of Mom's head in his jaws and was holding her face down in the water. I felt her terror, her utter helplessness in the face of being drowned or mauled or both. I knew that even if the bear released her for a moment, she wouldn't be able to escape because she doesn't know how to swim.

Her submerged body was motionless in the bear's grip but I could tell she was pleading with me to save her. I tried to think of ways to get the bear away from her so she could breathe, but everything I could think of seemed more dangerous than doing nothing. If I threw stones at the bear, he might get angry and clamp his jaws tighter around her head rather than release her. If I jumped into the water to reach her, he would probably kill me as well as her.

I knew that each second I delayed brought her closer to drowning. I didn't know which was worse—doing something that would probably result in my dying with her or letting her drown thinking I hadn't even tried to help. The conflict between wanting to save myself and not wanting to abandon her was overwhelming, and I awoke with the most intense feeling of terror and pity I have ever felt in my life, waking or sleeping.

Going back to sleep was unthinkable. I got up and went down to the kitchen. A feeling of hopelessness, of sickening personal failure, stayed with me for hours. I have never before had a dream in which my mother's life was in danger. . . .

Edina, Minn.
Wednesday, September 4
Last night, after learning Mom's tumor was malignant, I began packing for an indefinite stay in Minnesota. "I want my daughter," Mom said, planting a new phrase deep in my heart. I promised her I would be there by noon today and booked a 10:00 A.M. flight out of Newark. I packed and worried into the middle of the night, then set the alarm for 6:00 A.M., allowing enough time for the two-hour drive to the airport. When I awoke at 8:00 A.M. and realized I would miss the plane, bolts of lightning traveled through my veins. I booked a later flight, called Mom, lied and drove the Taconic Parkway at the speed of my heartbeat, ready to defy any state trooper who dared to come between me and my guilt.

On the plane, I kept thinking of something that has worried me since my brother Mike's first call last Tuesday. I have never been able to stand the sight of Mom in pain. I respond to it bodily. If she burns her hand on the iron, I wince. If she coughs, my chest heaves. Once, when we were shopping together in downtown Evanston, Mom tripped on a crack in the sidewalk and smashed headfirst into the pavement. My whole body started tingling, and when I saw the fright in her eyes, I almost fainted. The right half of her face looked broken, caved in, and I lied when she asked me if there was a mirror in the shoe store where we waited for an ambulance. I remember the effort I made to keep looking at her, as if there was nothing wrong, as if her beauty was intact.

I have witnessed only a few, rare accidents, spaced over decades of her healthy life. I have never had to repress, or even think about, my body's impulsive identification with hers. How will I react now that the threats to her are so much more extreme? What help will I be, what comfort can I give, if I am simply the mirror of her suffering? I wonder if all daughters feel this. Do we all have to go through a second weaning?

On the drive from the airport Mike and Dad told me more about the treatment the medical center is recommending for Mom. The first step is surgery, not to remove the tumor but to expose it directly to the highest possible dose of electron-beam radiation. As soon as she recovers from surgery, she will receive daily radiation treatments, delivered externally, for five weeks. She will also need a nerve block to control pain, because even if the tumor is rendered inactive by the radiation, it will still be there as a fibrous mass exerting pressure on nerves close to her spinal column. When Mom asked if any other follow-up treatment would be necessary, the oncologist said, "No, just routine checkups every six months for the first two years." Dad says "first two years" were the sweetest words he ever heard. . . .

Rochester, Minn.
Thursday, September 19
We left the hospital this morning with a few days' supply of codeine and a round of cheery good-byes from the nurses. The

farewells seemed inadequate, perhaps inevitably so. From the moment Mom was admitted to the hospital, these nurses became the most important people in the world. She depended on them initially for comfort, and ultimately for survival; in the first post-operative days, when her body literally could not function without them, we demanded that their concern for her be as profound as her dependence on them. We expected compassion as our due and we got it. Not until we were leaving did I realize how much we had asked of the nurses, and how much they had given. And yet, at parting, there was no time to acknowledge that extreme experience had been shared. There were, as always, new patients, new urgencies, new families demanding to be treated as the most important people in the world. And so we exchanged those inadequate, cheery good-byes. They pretended that Mom is all better now, which she isn't, and we pretended that their's was simply a job well done, which it wasn't. My respect for good nurses is boundless.

Doctors are another matter. No doctor even came by to discuss what special care Mom might need at home, and no prescriptions had been authorized. We would have left without even an aspirin if I hadn't insisted upon something for the pain that still burns in Mom's back.

Before leaving the hospital, Mom took codeine to help her through the two-hour drive home. As she sat in a wheelchair on the pavement outside the hospital entrance, Dad lowered the front passenger seat of his Renault into a reclining position, and we placed pillows against the seat to support Mom's distressed lower back. We used an overnight case as a footstool, hoping raised legs would put less strain on her still-healing incision. The move from wheelchair to car caused a few loud groans, but once Mom was settled, with a pillow clutched against her abdomen and blankets up to her ears, she was comfortable enough to take notice of the rain clouds that stretched from Rochester to Minneapolis. . . .

Glenco Mills, N.Y.
Thursday, October 10
I just returned from the fish hole, where I sat for hours on my double-trunked log peering into clear water. I saw a large fish emerge head first from under the carpet of fallen leaves that covers the stream bed. He looked like he was giving birth to himself, wiggling his way out of the earth full grown. I also saw a molting crayfish scuttle across the bottom and take cover under a maple leaf.

Two small fish, about four inches long, seemed to be playing with each other. They are, I suppose, too young to mate but their movements reminded me of the lizards I watched mating on the patio in Italy this summer. One fish would swim up to the side of another, and when he was exactly parallel to the other fish, sideswipe him. The sideswipe would knock them apart, and both fish quickly circled back for another collision. It looked very like the soccer drill in which two players stand side by side, jump into the air and butt shoulders. The butting would be repeated four or five times in quick succession, until one of the fish gave up and darted away. A couple minutes later, they would repeat the cycle.

At other times the two fish seemed to sniff each other's tails, like dogs do, or stroke one another with a slow swish of delicate tail, like cats. A larger fish flipped on its side and seemed to scratch itself against the leaves on the bottom of the stream. It was almost as if the presence of leaves in their world made the fish behave like land creatures for a day. Every other time I spied on them from my perch on the fallen sycamore, they swam without touching each other.

Tuesday, October 15
Mom had her first radiation treatment today. She said it was "scary." She must lie absolutely still on a hard, narrow slab, which is then raised several feet in the air. She is not scared of falling. What frightens her is the sound of technicians literally running for cover as she is being lofted toward the source of radiation. She will take this ride five days a week for the next five weeks. . . .

Tuesday, April 1
Yesterday, I decided to try out my new hip boots in preparation for the opening of trout season today. The boots are heavy, and you strap them on with canvas knee braces inside the boot as well as by straps extending from the top of the boot to belt loops. This keeps them securely on my legs, but it also means I'll have two fifty-pound weights strapped to my body if they should fill with water.

With boots on, I lumbered through the yard and down the path to the stream behind the house. Last spring the path led to a rocky strip of beach from which you could enter the stream in ankle-deep water. But now the stream is so swollen with melted snow that the beach is an island separated from the bank by several feet of fast-flowing water. I stepped in, and although the water only reached mid-calf, I had a hard time keeping my balance. Even in the ankle-deep water on the other side of the island, it was hard to keep my footing. Whenever I raised a boot off the streambed, the rushing water carried it a foot downstream. It felt like moon walking, except that I knew gravity would reassert itself if I slipped.

Walking upstream was impossible, and the only way to make safe progress downstream was to slide my foot along the rocky bottom until it found the next firm footing. In knee-deep water, the force of the stream pounding against my legs was so great that I had to struggle to remain standing. One slight slip would have sent me on a long, bumpy, boot-bound ride downstream to safer, shallower waters or to fatally deep ones.

That prospect didn't appeal, so I slogged my way back to the bank wondering why trout-fishing deaths were not a seasonal epidemic. It had taken all my strength and attention to stay upright, and I wasn't fishing. How would it be with a fishing rod in hand, and my concentration focused on the hunt?

On the local television news tonight, they said dangerously high water had kept a lot of fishermen out of the streams. Personally, I needn't have worried. There were no fish to distract me from boot management today. I started at the fish hole, using one of Dad's homemade nymphs on my fly rod, but without the sycamore trunk spanning the stream and slowing the water, the fish hole is less of a pool. It's become a stretch of water too fast-flowing and turbulent for fish to laze about in. After several dozen casts produced only a fingerling, I moved downstream to the bridge, where I had no better luck. Since there is no insect life on the stream yet for my flies to imitate, I didn't really expect any smart fish to strike, but I hoped for an ignorant stocked trout or two. . . .

Friday, April 18
Following Zack and Merc's advice, I tried fishing in the pools at the base of the dam behind the Kimberly-Clark Mill today. It didn't seem a very romantic spot to fish, but I figured if it's good enough for trout, it's good enough for me. I walked across the employee parking lot with fly rod in hand and clambered down

the steep bank on a path worn through poison ivy to an outcropping of rock about fifteen feet wide and thirty feet long. The roar of the Roe/Jan plunging over the dam drowned out the hum of the mill's generators, but the frothing spray of the waterfall also made it difficult to cast into the side pools that were my targets. I nearly hooked myself several times when the force of the spray whiplashed the line back in my face. Finally I discovered that a low side-arm cast brought the fly to rest on the pool instead of me. Even there the water swirled so fast that the fly was instantly sucked into a vortex and then spit up into the air yards away in imitation of no creature in its right mind. My only hope was that the trout in these pools were too dizzy to be discriminating.

Pulling the line in to make my fifth cast, I found a stunned eleven-inch brown trout in my possession. The tug of the currents against my line was so great I hadn't even known he was taking a ride on my hook. It wasn't brilliant gamesmanship on my part, but still it was a respectable-size fish and I decided to keep him around for a while, in case I caught another and had enough to offer the friend I'd invited for dinner. Instead of threading him onto a stringer, I cleverly put him in one of the water-filled crevices on outcropping of rock from which I was casting. Nature's minnow bucket, I thought, from which I could return him unharmed to the stream or take him home.

A few minutes later I hooked another trout, this time knowingly, and I let it play the line in sportsmanlike fashion. When I landed him, I gently carried his ten inches to the crevice where I had left the first fish, thinking my evening's menu was settled. But the first fish was gone. I shrugged and returned the second fish to the stream, figuring my odds against catching a third fish in the same spot were impossibly high.

I resumed casting just to pass the time and began to wonder

how that first fish managed to escape from the crevice. I set my rod down and returned to look for clues. On hands and knees I peered into the still water and saw a suspicious bulge in the silt at the bottom of the crevice. I reached into the water with my right hand and a cloud of mud exploded around my fingers. When the mud settled I saw my trout shuttling back and forth across the three-foot length of the crevice. Every time I grabbed, he dove straight to the bottom and stirred up a mud storm that left me in zero visibility. The water was only a foot deep, but that trout knew how to work every cubic inch of it.

I was so intent on our battle of wills that I failed to notice an audience had gathered. A dozen mill workers on coffee break had taken positions on a catwalk spanning the Roe/Jan about twenty-five yards downstream from me. The noise of the falls prevented me from hearing what they said as they gestured in my direction, but I could imagine the gist of it, and I knew I didn't have the protection of anonymity, because one of the men on the catwalk was Clara's husband, who no doubt informed the others I was the lady who bought his mother-in-law's house.

I waved and smiled, hoping they might arrive at a reasonable explanation for my behavior, then I returned to my task, which was, in fact, to save the fish. Personally, I couldn't have cared less if he lived out the rest of his life in that crevice, but I feared it would be a short, unhappy life unless I rigged up an aerator and brought him food every day. The problem was the trout still thought of me as his enemy and I knew there was no way of talking him out of it.

Bare-handed lunging clearly didn't work. I considered tying on my tastiest fly and flicking it daintily into the crevice, but it was too late in the game for that. I looked about me for a solution and spotted a plastic carton, the kind that might once have contained a half-pound of coleslaw, littering the bank. I fetched it, rinsed it in the stream and hovered above the crevice awaiting my moment.

When the trout paused to rest at the narrow end of the crevice, I plunged and scooped up his tail. He wriggled free, but before he could slap the bottom, I scooped again and caught him head first in the carton. Grabbing his tail with my free hand, I carried him, half-in/half-out of the carton, to the pool, where, in my haste to free him before he flapped out of my grip into another crevice, I slipped on the wet rocks and slid into the water with him. An adrenaline rush of fear shot through me before my feet hit a ledge of rock and I found myself standing waist deep in the coldest water that ever lapped my thighs.

I climbed back onto the outcropping and thanked the powers that be at Kimberly-Clark for the brevity of their coffee breaks. On the short drive home, I passed Zack and Merc, who asked me if I had tried the pools by the mill yet. I said yes, I had just caught two twelve-inch brown trout there, and thanked them for the tip. They asked why I was shivering, but since they could see me only from the chest up, I left them wondering. . . .

Edina, Minn.
Friday, April 25
I hate Mom's doctors. When I arrived in Edina this morning, I found her thinner, frailer and in greater pain that at any time since her operation. Last week she went to the pain clinic expecting to discover an array of alternatives to drugs for the back pain her oncologist says is not caused by cancer; what she was offered was another nerve block, and she was so desperate for relief that she let them perform the procedure the next morning.

Now she is at home, taking mind-fogging doses of codeine to

blunt the same intense burning pain the first nerve block caused. Her weight is down to 105 again, she has very little appetite and barely enough strength to walk from one room to the next. She is surprised by her misfortune and sure, as always, that she'll "feel better tomorrow." She doesn't remember that it took six weeks to recover from the side effects of this "cure-all," and nobody at the medical center reminded her.

I understand why most of the doctors cannot spend any more time or emotion on their patients than they do. They are specialists trained to intervene at moments of crisis, to cut, to radiate, to alter chemistry, then move on to the next patient. But why is there no place in this elaborate medical system for sustained care of the human being who continues to feel the effects of the doctors' knives and beams and chemicals? Why must medicine feel so much like a hit-and-run accident? . . .

Ancram, N.Y.
Sunday, July 27
I am having trouble explaining trout fishing to my city friends. They think it either idleness or blood lust, and can't imagine why I spend so much time in its pursuit. When they visit, I equip them for the stream, but they are bored within twenty minutes and look at me very strangely when I return home hours after they've resorted to more fail-safe diversions, like porch sitting, book in hand.

They don't feel the fascination of a stream, but then, neither did I before I began fishing. Oh, I was dazzled by the flow and sparkle, but that can be taken in at first glance, and unless you're in the mood to be hypnotized, it's not enough to hold one's attention for long. I only began to see things when I tried to think like a trout. The game of hide-and-seek we play is so stacked in the trout's favor that I must be as alert and wily as my inferior senses allow just to catch sight of him. When I approach the stream, I must step softly or he will pick up the vibration of my footfalls on the bank, sent express from my boots through the water to him. On sunny days, I must notice where shadows fall, so I can hide my own among those cast by the trees, or he will know a large, ungainly creature has darkened his shimmering world.

Before entering the stream, I sit on the bank for a while to see what insects are swarming above the water. I turn over rocks in the streambed to see who's living there. I am not a strict imitationist, but if I can't approximate the size and shape, color and movement of something above, below or on the surface of the water, I might as well surrender my hopes for the day. I have tried expressionist flies, but they work only on expressionist fish, like bass, who will leap for any gaudy bauble when they're in the mood. Trout have more refined tastes.

Even a finicky trout must eat, though, and he can't expend more energy getting food than the food supplies, or he will waste away to nothing; he must find some quiet spot and let the food come to him. This knowledge is my only edge, so once in the stream, I scan the surface of the water for variations in its flow. I look for large boulders above and below the surface, for fallen logs and indentations in the bank, anything that interrupts the flow of the stream, creating pockets of still water on its downstream side where a trout can rest without struggling against the current. I approach such places with great stealth, staying in the shadows when possible, inching my boots along the slippery, moss-covered rocks of the streambed, checking in all directions for overhanging branches that might snag my fly before it reaches its target. Wind permitting, I try to cast my fly just upstream from where I suspect the trout will be so my tempting morsel will float right past him.

If my fly lands on the water more indelicately than a gnat would, the older, wiser, larger trout will let it pass and I'll never know what I've missed. There are no second chances with an experienced trout; the merest suspicion of a predator in the vicinity and he will not risk revealing his hideout by taking any insect, hand-tied or God-made, for hours. I might trick a six-inch native trout or even a ten-inch stocked trout, a newcomer to the stream raised in the sheltering walls of a hatchery, but to catch a veteran trout, twelve inches or more, I must be perfect, and I seldom am. I may move soundlessly through the water for twenty yards, stirring not a ripple as I approach a likely spot, and then stumble just as I'm about to cast, sending a tidal wave of warning to even the most innocent stockie. Or my wrist may betray me and shoot the line out so fast it slaps the surface of the water or lands in a spiraling jumble, as if I'd cast the web as well as the fly.

When I'm fishing well, my concentration is so intensely focused on the surface of the stream that I enter a kind of trance, from which I emerge startled by some sudden sound or change in light. I'll look up, as if just awakened from a dream, and see a great blue heron taking flight at my approach, the tips of his spindly legs lagging three feet behind his crested head, curled claws still skimming the surface of the water. One hazy afternoon, I looked up, reentered time and felt a sudden searing stab of fear. Day had departed unnoticed by me, and the last rays of the setting sun shot horizontally through the woods toward me like the beams of a motorcycle gang waiting in silent ambush.

Often, on clear days, I'll see a cardinal fly across the stream ahead of me, a streak of red against blue sky for an instant before he's lost again in the green world of the other bank. Every time, I think of the passage from Venerable Bede about the flight of the sparrow through the mead hall. Bede likened the sparrow's flight from door to door to the brevity of man's life on earth. I too am reminded of mortality, but, midstream on a sunlit day, I have no complaint. If the cardinal's flight from bank to bank were less fleeting, it would also be less glorious. Midstream, it seems all right to die; sickness is the sin. . . .

Saturday, November 8
Last night I dreamt that Dad and I were in a cemetery where Mom was buried. There was no plot to the dream, just a climate, strange to say, of contentedness. The cemetery was green and leafy and it seemed a fine place to be. Dad and I were smiling. There was a vivid sense of Mom's presence there, and of her contentment with her new home. In fact, the mood was almost what it would be if one of us were showing the other two the new house we had bought and everyone was pleased with the choice. In this case, the new home was hers, a dream reversal of my frustrated wish to show her mine.

Montevarchi, Italy
June 1987
I have my answer, at least for now. I don't find the living presence of my mother in memory, in photographs or anecdotes; I find her instead in moonlight and breezes. On August nights, I pretend shooting stars are signals sent from her to me. I am not talking about belief but the experience of consolation. Certain, unexpected sights or sensations console me the way the feel of familiar beads passing through thumb and forefinger might console someone else. I am thankful that my discovery of death coincided with my discovery of a new setting, thankful that death found me midstream, where the play of light on water makes me feel blessed.

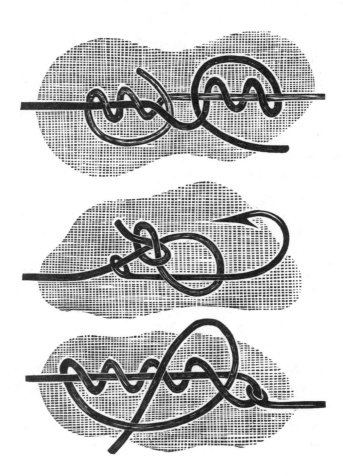

AILM TRAVLER

Run-Off

THE WORD passion comes from the Latin *passio*, to suffer. This spring during run-off I realized that fly fishing is about suffering and that it would always break my heart. I also know, even though it took many days and nights of a spring that held winter ransom and claimed half of summer, that for those of us who suffer our fly fishing passions, there is grace.

As with every passion, the story does not unfold simply. I live in northern New Mexico where the very existence of water is a contradiction. Not only are the fickle mountain seasons cruel to trout and fly fishers, fly fishing is an act of bearing witness to centuries of abuse to the ecosystems that create the riffles, pools and pocket water where I search for trout.

When I try to escape to meet my passion in the shadowed canyons and high secret lakes, I come face to face with the contradictions. I feel like the adversary every time I hook a trout and fight it out of its perfect holding place. Often the dice feel loaded —it is as though the places trout have left to hold are marked with fluorescent red ribbon. I begin to loathe catching fish.

But then there is that late spring morning when the insects appear early and the western fly catcher whistles before dawn— the passion hooks me and I'm helpless. I can smell the streams again, hear the river, feel the difference at last of breaking summer: the way the insects float aimlessly in the webby light and the trout rise innocently out of the shadows, perfectly fulfilled.

A sphere is a totality, a whole, and water will always attempt to form an organic whole by joining what is divided and uniting it in circulation. It is not possible to speak of the beginning or end of a circulatory system; everything is inwardly connected and reciprocally related. Water is essentially the element of circulatory systems.[1]

The landscape in which I live and fish is a series of ridges, basins, alpine forests, high desert canyons, ponderosa parks and mountain meadows formed by the southernmost reaches of the Rocky Mountains and the Colorado Plateau. It is a country of extremes. The dry high desert ecosystems through which our streams and rivers flow, thirst for and thrive on the mountain

---

1. *Sensitive Chaos*, Theodor Schwenk, Rudolf Steiner Press, London, 1965.

snows of winter, and they suck up the moisture quickly in the hot summers.

Trout fishing here is the art of tightrope walking those fleeting few days—moments sometimes—between run-off and drought. Winter is long, but run-off is the longest season of all.

Winter here in the mountains is hard. By mid-November the ice has irrevocably covered the creeks and locked away the trout. Everything is frozen. No more dappled waters, clouds of insects in the rising heat of the morning, no more hushed evening rises. The body closes down, blood thickens, and instead of adventures to unknown rivers, fretful journeys inward begin.

During the winter I dream about fishing. These are not wish-fulfillment dreams. Thinly disguised allegories, they nightmar-ishly tempt me, take me away to the pristine places I long for, and then cruelly subject me to lessons in suffering.

The places I long for: if I lived by an unsung river, if there were no fences, no No Trespassing signs; if the mountains rose up blanketed with forests and meadows and no roads marred them; if birds returned in droves in the spring; if the gleaming rivers were teeming with fish.

There is a particularly beautiful stretch of small highway west of here that runs through the meadows and forests of posted cattle lands. I ski and snowshoe that country in the winter when most of the highway is closed. In the spring I watch streams with names like Placer, Tusas, Nutrias and San Antonio gush down from the highlands and in the summer go almost dry as they are diverted to irrigate dryland pastures.

Last spring I saw a cowboy hunched over muddy, swollen Tusas Creek, watching the weir he had constructed out of chicken wire, waiting for it to fill up with trout. Across the road from his weir was an assortment of decaying log buildings, old trucks, a tractor and rake, and a house. At the turnoff to the place was an imposing log-pine gate in the shape of a gallows bearing the name DAD'S DREAM RANCH. Hanging there was a dummy of a man with a scrawled sign on the right: Not Responsible for Injuries While Trespassing, and a sign on the left: We Do Things the Old Way. I knew that in a few weeks, when the stream was low again, the cowboy would be making diversions out of orange tarp so that what was left of the creek could water his pastures.

In a dream I had this winter, a stream like the Tusas sparkled as it meandered through meadows lined with aspen. The sun glinted off the backs of cruising trout visible through the clear water. Right there by the highway, huge trout rose from beneath grassy undercut banks to take insects off the water in synchronous rings. I get out of my pickup, feel the breeze in my hair, the sun in my face, and realize that I don't have my fly rod with me.

Winter is long, but its gift is snow. In northern New Mexico our annual rainfall, which comes mostly during the rainy season in July, is a pittance, so we count on a good snowpack in the mountains. It's all we talk about as spring approaches. For farmers and gardeners in our valley snowpack means longer irrigation, especially for people downstream. For those with the passion, snowpack also means good flows, lots of insects, and spawning and growing trout.

Winter began early this year and lasted weeks longer than usual. I got more than restless, I was anxious. I dreamed about my fly rod, just my fly rod sitting there, leaning against a wall indoors. I wondered if as a child I longed to go fishing. In an old family album there is a picture of me wearing a buckskin jacket among the cedar trees, casting on a lawn covered with snow.

I spent a few weeks of many childhood summers on a small island, a three-acre slab of grown-over granite in the middle of an Adirondack lake, forested with tall white pines and strewn with blueberry and wintergreen bushes. It was the first place I ever fished. I used clam innards on a hook and string and dangled for bluegills off the dock.

The structures on the island—cabins, kitchen, boathouse—are more than a hundred years old; there is no electricity, but there are plenty of canoes and guideboats from which, four generations ago, my relatives caught immoral numbers of brook trout on the outlet river. You don't hear much about trout anymore. So this winter, when it seemed like I would never fish again, I became obsessed with the idea of going back there, as a fly fisher now, and finding them.

Then I had a dream. In the dream, the island was crisscrossed by underground streams which became intertwining creeks. It had been raining all day and I'd been inside the main cabin waiting for the weather to change.

Finally I go out to "peruse the fishing situation." I look down into the clear water, furtively, so I won't be seen by the trout. I am surprised at the size of the trout in there, brookies grown to sixteen to twenty inches—a rare sight. In another creek there are long bluefish and round redfish. Yet another creek is full of bluegills, sunfish and perch. Then it begins raining. I go inside to get my fishing stuff. When I come out again the streams are muddy and I can't fish.

Run-off anxiety.

As winter stretches into April I feel displaced, a back channel winding lost. Part of me is frozen, part of me is running wild, about to slide over a logjam waterfall. In desperation, at the first hint of a spring change, I take off.

I drive all over creation, into Colorado and out again into New Mexico, to fish a river where just before it slides into a canyon with posted signs, a fairly wild stretch passes through national forest. And even better, you can ford the river there and get to wilderness creeks beyond.

Twice I try to get to the ford, but the snow is too deep and the Forest Service has locked the gates to the primitive road. Finally one day I make it, driving down a tortuous, gullied, bare excuse for a road, to the ford. Cataracts of frothing muddy water funnel into the canyon. There are no banks to speak of on either side of the river from which to negotiate fishing, and it is obvious that nothing will be able to cross to the other side for at least a month. The smell of willows sagging with mud surrounds me, fierce winds slam my pickup door shut. It is dark when I get home.

A few weeks later I dreamed that I was about to ford the Rio Brazos, a brookie stream in the mountains just west of that ford, to get to the other side (which is always better fishing): I brake my pickup at the ford and look out at the rapids. The stream is as wide as the Mississippi River near my childhood home in Minnesota and like the Mississippi, it is deep enough for barges. A slick light glints off the whitecaps and I imagine the drowned hulls of trucks and cars swaying in the current at the bottom.

A warm spell in April. Grasses poke out shoots in my field; deer graze by the house, elk congregate by the marsh and visit the salt lick. The bluebirds return.

I drive to a river an hour and a half away—a short distance for a day trip around here. At the lower end the river has Game and Fish public access and is usually pretty fished out. Up river, boundaried by National Forest and wilderness, the river runs through private land. Year after year I have tried to fish this perfect sized, wadable river before the crowds arrive, but it is either too high at run-off or too low immediately after as the ranchers upstream open their diversion gates. Three years in a row I have been thwarted. This time, I think, I've hit it just right.

When I get there it is cloudy and cold. Portions of the access road are under water. I put on my waders and step into the slate-colored river. It begins to snow. I slap a hare's ear into a river of comatose trout. My fingers freeze, and still I cast that pitiful nymph. After a dangerously long period of denial, I finally pack up and go home.

If you want to actually catch fish during run-off, you have to use a nymph; there is no other way. The water is muddy and murky, and where there were once rocks and pocket water is a high running sheen that carries away every holding log, sweeper and dam. Run-off scours stream beds and rips away stream banks. But we know that trout are holding in places we can come close to imagining with our hare's ears, double-hackled peacocks, pheasant tails and woolly buggers.

But this winter I rounded up all the various, multihued and textured nymphs I had ever tied and put them in a box marked "nymphs." I decided I didn't want to fish nymphs anymore. Just like that.

I don't want to be encased, a crawler, a clinger, struggling to break surface, weighted, sunk, scraping the bottom, torpedoing through darkness. I want to watch the story unfold, I want to play in dappled light, in the foam line, arc over grasses and into pools of fading stars.

The passion. Sometimes it's not about catching fish, but rather about a continuing natural order in the cosmos—something I can peg my world onto, something I can count on. Observing and suffering through run-off, as it begins its trickling origins from melting patches on subalpine slopes and rivulets in spring bog meadows, to the moment when it forms into streams and finally into rivers, is to observe a circulatory system that signifies the humming, synchronous meshing of parts without which there would be no life.

The fact is, if there were no run-off, or worse, if run-off came only between 3:00 P.M. and 6:00 P.M., we would be in trouble. Run-off is manifest destiny's worst nightmare: chaos; savage nature; uncontrolled, undammed, unchecked wildness. If there are still trout, its because the system is working and we know the source.

There is a river I discovered by accident a couple of years ago. I don't know where its headwaters are, but I have hiked to it from two confluences, small creeks near the headwaters that feed the river as it runs its course through a cattle ranch and then drops through a narrow canyon, guarded by nettles and inaccessible except by wading.

This river is different from others I know. In the summer it is amber-colored; the distinctive rocks and boulders that form the necessary pools, falls and pockets in its moderate flow are smooth and gray. As you descend into the canyon the boulders become monstrous and the pools grottos, perfect for swimming and for surprising bigger browns and rainbows on light-colored flies.

You can see trout cruise the grottos in midday, and in the afternoon, sit on a bank to watch small rainbows do flips in the air as large mayflies hatch. Stone-fly skeletons cover the rocks. During early morning and late evening mayfly hatches, rises continuously ring the slower water. I have invented and tied more flies for this river than any other.

I have always fished this river at low water in midsummer, but this year I wanted to see it in the spring during high water— and be there when the first mayflies hatched.

In early May I drive an old logging road inland. About two miles before the turnoff to the hike to the river my way is blocked by snow and puddled moors. The ridge above the ranch is covered with snow.

Two weeks later I try again and barely make it. The black mud sucks at my tires as I maneuver the road. When I get out of my pickup I can hear the roar of the river in the distance. I hike down the hill through patches of snow, marveling how the raging river below dwarfs the spare alpine landscape in its writhing, frothing course.

I arrive at the confluence. The normally tiny feeder creek that winds invisibly from the ridge through alders and pine is a muddy cascade I can see for miles tumbling down the mountainsides. The banks of the stream, left bare by cattle, crumble as the water tears at the curves and washes away the earth around stunted willows. The river is so high that it seems to lift itself out of the riverbed, pushing aside everything in its path. The roar pulses like heartbeats pushing blood through arteries.

I hike in again a week later. The water is not quite as high but it is still cold and muddy and there are no visible flying insects except a couple of midges. Long grasses at the high-water mark lie flattened in the mud, inclined as if in a current; driftwood branches and bleached-out twigs are heaped up along the shore like colonies of log cabins leveled by a tornado. Downriver whole trees have piled up, forming dams with tantalizing new pools behind them.

On my way out, with my rod still in its case, I notice that the backwater channels created by the run-off have withered away from the river and formed ponds where little white flowers are pushing up through the mud along the edges. A small trout, stranded in one of the clear pools, darts under a lone rock when I pass by.

> *So when the Nile, the stream with seven mouths*
> *recedes from the soaked fields and carries back*
> *its waters to the bed they had before,*
> *and slime, still fresh, dries underneath the sun,*
> *the farmers, turning over clods, discover*
> *some who are newly born, who've just begun*
> *to take their forms, and others who are still*
> *unfinished, incomplete—they've not achieved*
> *proportion; and indeed, in one same body,*
> *one part may be alive already, while*
> *another is a lump of shapeless soil.*
> *For, tempering each other, heat and moisture*
> *engender life: the union of these two*
> *produces everything. Though it is true*
> *that fire is the enemy of water,*
> *moist heat is the creator of all things:*
> *discordant concord is the path life needs.*

—Ovid, *The Metamorphoses*

I've always thought of my life as a river. Sometimes I feel a destiny in its course, unpredictably predictable in its twists and turns. So it was on one of those frustrating non-fishing trips to the hare's ear snowstorm river that a man drove up the road on his ATV and we got to talking. It turned out that he was the owner of land on a stretch of the river a number of miles up the road—the paradise beyond the gate I had wanted to climb over for years. His forebears go back so many generations they are names on the topo map.

I return there in July, at his invitation, with a fly box full of bushy elk-haired flies. When I get to the end of the road, he is on his backhoe, repairing a bridge that had been washed out during run-off. The meadows are humming with insects; flowers scatter colors over the waving grasses. My first cast to the leading edge of a boulder yanks me to my knees. I begin to slough off winter. I fish until I lose a yellow stimulator in the grass and realize I am bone tired and it is time to go.

Sitting on a rock in the hot evening shadows, breaking down my rod, I look across at the dark fir and watch a balloon of huge dark mayflies rising and falling above the surface of the stream. Clouds of fluttering caddis hover around the alders along the bank. The hiss of the water rises as the shadows slide toward me across the river. Another troupe of pale yellow mayflies, smaller than the others, begins a dance above the water. Hatches like fireworks. I watch them until the shadows cool and all that's left is the sound of the water.

Grace. The pull of earthly passions and the compelling, spiraling course of rivers is a balancing act. I want to feel my body as a river, with its tributaries to the spine and alluvial streams coursing outward; a witness trying to find her bearings, bearing witness to the waters that hold her in thrall.

There is a place I inevitably go back to as a touchstone for that feeling—the first place I ever fished in New Mexico. It is a high basin formed by a snowy ridge circling from east to west, where three streams, each from a different direction, flow down through achingly beautiful meadows to form a larger stream that disappears into a forest and reappears again in a small open valley. It's a place where dreams come true.

Last fall near the end of the day I discovered that beavers had changed the valley below the forest by creating the largest dam I had ever seen. Behind it were a series of ponds and rivulets below which the stream found its way into the old channel. It was getting late, and it was hunting season. First thing next spring, I said.

All winter I imagined how it would be, sneaking up behind that dam and casting blind into the big pond. I even knew what fly I would tie, something with peacock on it, I decided.

I couldn't get into the basin again until June because of the snow. When I do, blue flag is carpeting the meadows, and warbling thrushes echo through the aspen glades. I can hear the hushed roar of water in the distance as I hike down—but the creeks are clear.

The beavers' dam had made it through run-off and the ponds are filled to the brim. I crouch and crawl and slither along the dam, put some slack in my line and send it out over the mud-daubed branches onto the glassy surface. Splash. Leap. I stand up and play the speckled brookie, landing it before it tangles us in the dam, and flip it off the hook back into its glassy pool again.

I fish all day—in the morning the beavers' flooded willow valley, later back up into the basin meadows. I fish up one of the forks and down another, seeking brookies in the undercut banks, bends, and pools at the roots of occasional blue spruce; casting humpies and Adams'—nothing fancy or obscure.

Evening comes too soon. A breeze tosses the grasses, a thrush chimes from the woods. I pack up my stuff—this time because the day has been perfect. I hike back up the long hill out of the basin and stop to get my breath at the edge of the forest. Looking down at the silvery moon streams glinting their way from the snowy ridge to that place by the boulders where I have just witnessed a passion play of insects, water and fish, I feel as if finally my circulatory system has been replaced by streams.

MARGOT PAGE

The Island

THE ATLANTIC OCEAN off Cape Cod is virtually boiling with fish, the brownish striped bass rolling slowly on their sides as they gulp the bait they have trapped on the surface. A layer of bluefish slash just underneath. Aglint in the high summer sun, sea gulls hover excitedly twenty feet above the water, one to a fish, dropping to the surface when they see a choice available morsel of baitfish.

Gleeful shouts pepper our twenty-one-foot craft as we stagger for balance in the pitch and rock of the waves. The fish move toward us and then away in predatory packs, marked by gulls and the agitated surface. In between frenzied moments of their activity, we wait at attention, scanning the surface of the water intently, heads swiveling. We're not looking at one another: all eyes are on the gulls and the water. We hold our fly lines at the ready.

Tom and I have brought Brooke along—now seven and a half, too smart for empty promises, too young for no reward—with the tantalizing promise of a boat ride to a tiny "desert island" off the Cape.

Our captain is Tony Biski, a burly, enthusiastic convert to fly fishing, about which he says, "Fly fishing is an art, something to do while you're fishing." Today he is taking us to the flats off Monomoy Point, the thin finger of sand pointing south from the Cape's elbow, home to seabirds, dunes, and many sea disasters of yore. But while we're coming off the high tide, we detour to The Rip where he's just received radio reports of blitzing fish.

My arm is firmly around Brooke's tubby, colorful life preserver. Her Barbie dangles from her hand as we skim over the high tide which covers the miles of undulating white sand we will later walk. Approaching the ocean side of Monomoy we can smell the distinctive oil slick produced by baitfish being shredded, and see gulls circling and diving—two sure indicators of large groups of working fish.

While Tony controls the boat, trying not to drift over the path of the fish, we swiftly lift our rods out of the keepers. Within a couple of casts, Tom hooks and lands two fish, and then—after a drawn-out fight into the backing—lands a twenty-pound striper. I, too, quickly hook a heavy fish and can feel him shaking his head against the line. Pulling him in, we see the flashes of blue—he is a large bluefish—just before he shakes himself one last time and bites off my tippet with his razored teeth.

We wait in a momentary calm, and Tony repositions the boat to where the gulls are working. The brown rolls start in waves towards us, a liquid earthquake, the gulls again fluttering above. Not used to a stripping basket, I have elected to leave my line free and as a result familiarize myself with every proturberance in Tony's boat. As I am having trouble casting any distance with the 9-weight rod into the wind, Tony suggests I use his 8-weight with a sinking line. Instantly my range improves and the deep ache in my shoulder disappears, but because of my excitement, I still cast badly and miss.

Seeing striped bass in such healthy profusion after the decline of the seventies and eighties is wild and exhilarating. They arc in chopping circles, swirls of beige backs breaking the surface as they twist and turn in deceptively lazy vicious packs. Daytime fishing is, obviously, different from night fishing, because here you can see the fish moving up from the murky depths or prowling along the surface. You can see the take or kick yourself about what you're missing. Of course, night fishing has its particular compensation: the sea's neon phosphorescence lights up the stripers as if they're electric.

And then there's always the indigo night.

By this time, Brooke's patience is beginning to fray. We have sold this expedition to her based on an island of sand and that is what she wants to see *right now*. Nearly an hour of this pitching and rolling is enough. She begins to complain. "You two are fishing maniacs," she cries with only marginal humor.

Fish are boiling towards us again and our attention is

diverted from her crisis. We cast furiously into the watery chaos, hooking or missing as the case may be, forgetting about the small, unhappy member of our quartet. Soon, we hear the sound of pointed foot stamping, harumphing, and covert groans. We are too preoccupied to respond. Tom hooks a huge striper and our yells of delight set Brooke off in the opposite direction. Never one to hide her feelings, she shouts as loudly, "I WANT TO GO TO THE ISLAND NOW!" But my attention shifts to Tom whose face is wreathed with joy as the giant bass runs down into the depths. He sets about bringing it in. Brooke will have no part of it. "NOOO MORE FISSSHHHHINNNGGG!"

To fend off impending disaster, Tom, at the same time he reels in his prize, launches into a long and complicated story involving a cockatiel at a pet store who has amazing adventures. As soon as she hears the magic words, "Once upon a time," Brooke instantly settles into her rapt listening mode, but she is still suspicious enough of her good fortune to give no quarter. When Tom pauses to reel and pump the line and marvel at his luck for a few seconds, Brooke registers immediate vocal displeasure, and Tom resumes, seamlessly, the meandering thread of his story. When the fish is landed and released, the cockatiel's saga continues through my search for my fish ("No, Brooke, we *can't leave* until Mommy gets *her* fish," Tom explains.)

Mercifully, I finally hook and land a small striper, about twelve pounds, who takes me into the short backing. Tony, the captain, has been feeling the strain. He flicks a drop of sweat from his brow and grins happily. We take a couple of photographs, release the fish, and Tom gives me a kiss and formal congratulations on my first daytime striper. Brooke is moaning insistently. We zoom quickly back to the flats where the tide is receding.

"You've been spoiled, Margot, really spoiled," Tom teases with satisfaction. "You've seen it as good as it gets."

The high tide is on the wane, leaving crescent pillows of fawn-colored sand islands that turn white as they dry. On the horizon the emerald dunes that line Monomoy lend the seascape dimension and color under the reassuring blue dome of this enormous summer sky. Old fishing weirs spike in the distance, like startling, thin, tall fences sticking out of the ocean, grandfathered down in families through the area's salty legacy.

We jump out of the boat into knee-deep, clear ocean water. I strip to my bathing suit and anorak and wade over the firm flats, grateful to sink my feet into the fine, sugar sand. If you didn't know you were on the Massachusetts coast, you could be persuaded this was the Caribbean, so clear is the water, so smooth and white the sand.

In the distance, Tony stalks the flats like a muscular, nut-brown bear, his keen green eyes looking seaward always. Over on the other side of the island, Tom has flipped his stripping basket over his shoulder and is heading away; in one hand he carries his rod and with the other holds the hand of a little girl with a blonde braid who wears a shocking pink bathing suit and carries a bright blue pail, both colors visible at long distance. They range further, getting smaller and vaguer, one looking for shells and crabs, one looking for fish. Ocean treasures. When we leave later that afternoon, Tony tells me he has named this little island for Brooke.

Several days later, Brooke is invited to play at the beach with friends. At this point in our vacation week, I am numbed from the medical problems of my father, a widowed stroke victim, who lives on the Cape year-round. We have come to visit him only to discover him in medical crisis. Though I have other things on my mind than fishing during this short reprieve from my unofficial nursing duty, I am drawn—hollow as I feel at the moment—to the water. We go again to the sea.

This day we hit low tide right on the nose. Tom and I are now enjoying the company of two Tonys, our captain again, Tony Biski, and our artist friend Tony Stetzko, who in 1981 held the world's record for a surf-caught striper (seventy-three pounds). The sheet of water on the flats we had skimmed over three days ago has now receded, leaving acres of white, rippled sand. Before Tony B. finishes anchoring the boat in the remaining tide, I plunge into the clean, warm ocean, readying my rod with one hand and adjusting a waist pack around my neck with the other.

Shouted instructions drift on the wind behind me as the two Tonys rig up their tackle. Tom is out of the boat too, ranging wordlessly and rapidly out to the far flats through the knee-deep water. Tony S. strides out through the water calling eagerly to me, "You're too far, come in on this side of the slough, they're all in here." A pause, then a shout, "LOOK AT THEM . . . SEE THOSE HUGE SHADOWS, THERE THEY GO!"

Behind me there is a close splash, and I hear it and Tony doesn't. I whirl and see the boil and cast and instantly nail a large creature. Plunging, the beast runs out for a while, then eventually turns and bites the hook off.

We wait and shuffle along the slough, this being apparently a slow day on the flats, and Tony teaches me: *See the birds working over there, see the dark edge near the light band, that's where they're coming in, going after the bait, pushing them to-*

ward the beach. They like to rub their bellies on the sand, so they come in shallow. They're coming right in. OH, LOOK AT THEM, OH, HERE THEY COME, GET READY, GET READY, THEY'RE MONSTERS, OVER HERE, RIGHT IN FRONT OF . . . (cast, cast, cast, strip, strip, strip).

OH . . . Oh . . . oh . . . there they go. . . . Tall and lean, Tony has long, dark Botticelli curls and a small, somewhat dashing scar on his cheek from a boating accident. A friend to all, he boyishly strides the Cape beaches like a great, excited heron.

We walk along the exposed tidal flats of this broad ocean floor, following the little rivers that flow through channels in the dead-low water. Stripers, blues, and maybe bonito are cruising along these miniature rivers, the Tonys explain to us, dining on nature's conveyer belt of sand eels and baitfish.

We come to the convergence of tidal flows where we catch a tidy number of stripers, fishing our striper patterns like nymphs, releasing them all after admiring their size or coloration. Someone brings me a live sand dollar to admire. I had only ever seen their bleached skeletons—and I place the brown-flanneled disk back in the ocean to, I hope, find a mate and make more sand dollars.

Then we amble back to our original starting position before the quickly incoming tide dissipates the still-feeding stripers off Brooke's Island's shores. While we walk back, Tony S. tells me how once he was so excited casting to a night blitz of fish that he dislocated his shoulder—which didn't deter him from completing the evening's fishing. Now *that's* a fishing maniac.

By the time we reach the island, my intense need to catch fish has subsided. I have another mission.

After casting without success for a while, I wade back to the anchored boat by myself, grab a sandwich, soda, and a towel, and run back over the humped sand bar to where my carefully placed rod is about to get engulfed by wavelets. Safely repositioning it in a cradle of dark seaweed near the apex of the island, I spread my towel on the white sand of this crescent island and eat my lunch.

In the distance stand the optimistic, hazy figures of the men poised at the ready in the shimmering ocean. Around me, dunlins and yellowlegs twitter and scurry. As I relax, only the sound of the waves and the wind and the birds fill my ears.

Now it is time.

I am overwhelmed trying to spread myself around to all those who need me—my father on the Cape, my husband and daughter, my work. Two households to run, an expanded team of nurses and home-health aides' schedules to keep track of. How to keep my father safe and honor his wishes to stay at home when he needs twenty-four-hour nursing care?

At this moment, I just want to run away. The nightmares of aides not showing up have made even my nights heavy. I can't get away from the image of my father's jaw clenched in pain, the helplessness of his frail body. The stuffiness of that old, hot, whaling captain's house. I wait for the weariness, the confusion, the sadness to be washed out of me by the only salve I know.

The sand crystals coat my hand where it lies on the beach, the terns mew and cry, the sun warms my shoulders. There is a deep throb of a boat on the horizon and the sound of the waves nurturing constancy as they throw themselves on the beach one after the other. Here, on this little island, miles from the mainland, there is no talking, no demands, no decisions I have to make. I am responsible, at this instant, only for myself. Not a hu-

man figure in sight except for the three sympathetic and somewhat protective men who have brought me here and are now
gathered on the faraway boat to eat their lunch.

This is my oasis. Brooke's Island. The island of a young girl
in a pink bathing suit with a bright blue pail, her blonde hair
shining like a beacon.

Here, a bit of wonder returns to pierce my depression. Here,
the breeze begins to blow and cleanse. The distant thrum of the
boat engine, the calling of the plovers, the sandpipers, the steady
fall of the waves, start to nibble at the mounting chaos of schedules, urinals, emergency trips to the pharmacy for gauze, saline,
rubber gloves and medicine.

I stand up and walk the receding perimeters of this white
crescent island, now a mere patch curving out of the encroaching,
resolute ocean. I mark off my territory, reclaiming myself from
within my father's slow demise. No one is watching me, I am
alone. My companions are back out on the flats, ever hopeful,
ranging like a small pack of benign wolves.

He's suffered enough. Twenty-two years of paralysis.

The rivers of salt water are now slowly narrowing the spit of
white sand. Little lapping rivers turn into wide ones, then become bays, and then merge with the ocean. Soon the foam will
touch my toes and I will move further up the island.

I can't fill my mind enough with the seascape, the radiating
light, the liquid sounds of the sea. But random thoughts intrude:
images of the icy February ocean ahead. Worries from life back
in Vermont. How in an hour we shall have to leave and I fear I
won't be able to return to fish these flats for another year.

Eight long-necked cormorants skim low over the water's

surface. They line the tidal islands, some with wings extended, frozen in mid-flap as they dry their feathers. Sandpipers hurry by me along the water's edge like race walkers in the park, beady dark eyes darting nervously. It's gratifying to note their healthy populations.

All of us have our own rivers, I remind myself, with their own beginnings and endings. I am alone on mine, as is my father. I stand in awe of the wonder of circumstance and the mysteries of our lives.

Tom splashes over with a bottle of mint iced tea and some sugar wafers. "They're *killing* them out in the rip! Wanta go or stay here?"

I elect to stay and he and the two Tonys speed out toward the Atlantic with lots of large hand-waves and big smiles.

I look around. Now I can be by myself on the planet, for this briefest of moments in time. Maybe they'll forget me and I'll have to spend the night on the island.

This idea makes me excited and nervous.

I will bundle up in my windbreaker and towel. I have a Tootsie Pop, Snapple, and a pack of Kleenex in my waist pack, along with a juicy book, pen, and fat notebook. I will watch the glorious Cape Cod sun go down on my now-tiny island of twenty square feet. Then I will huddle and wait for the Perseid meteor shower, the silver dashes flashing so fast in the inky canopy you're not sure you even saw them.

With my rod and only one fly, I will catch a small bluefish, eat sushi, chew on some seaweed. Suck on the last of the lemon drops. Morning will come, a sunrise of indisputable hope and renewal. The striped bass will roil in, just for me, and I shall cast, catch, and release these great creatures from the ocean. Later in the day, the Coast Guard will pick me up on my deserted island, sunburned, thirsty, and I shall have been cleansed by the meteors, the salt winds, the cry of the terns. My fears of death and loss will have been swept away, and I will be ready to return to my father.

I am alone. Peace wraps me like an airy miracle. Slow and light.

Some time later, the wavelets converge and move more rapidly up the white sand, devouring several inches a minute. I notice a more insistent tone to the waves as they get closer. I pick up my gear and move it into the very middle of the exposed sand with a faint feeling of alarm. My crescent island is becoming a fingernail. I am under the assumption that this island stays dry but we are still two hours away from peak high tide. What if this is an abnormal tide? What if my whole island gets swallowed and my companions haven't returned?

I succumb to a brief moment of panic and then happen to glance over to a corner of the island where two seagulls are standing on a tiny crescent island of their own. At the same instant my eyes alight on them, their sliver of land is being washed over by the first waves. The gulls, looking calmly out to sea, stand knee-deep in the rising tide and then confidently strut about their drowned island.

Again, I patrol my island as the tide comes up. I can measure its width in number of footsteps and as I walk, I notice that I am not altogether alone. A strange speedboat with one lone occupant has been making a couple of large circles around my island, watching me with craned neck, I now realize. I mildly speculate on what kind of weapon a graphite fly rod would make.

As I complete my tour with hands clasped behind my back,

watching my feet making prints in the sand, Tom and the two Tonys suddenly appear, surfing in fast to the island on a big boat wake with anxious looks on their faces. It turns out they couldn't see me from afar, and when they finally spotted my vertical figure on the horizon, it looked as if I was engulfed by water, with that lone boat circling like a shark.

I also learn that my island does *not* remain dry at high tide.

We head for home. The guys are still talking with fevered interest about where the bass are, what and why they do what they do. Tony S. enthuses about plans to bring a mask and a raft the next time, so he "can swim down one of the rivers of eel grass right next to the bass." As we gather speed, I look behind me at Brooke's Island. A vessel in full sail moves majestically behind it as the slim patch of sand disappears in the waves.

We hit the rougher water, banging and slamming hard into the waves, the wind whipping strings of my hair into my mouth. Each hard satisfying crash pounds away the remnants of my depression. The pointed white nameless ghosts of a sailing regatta line the haze on the horizon. One has capsized.

Suddenly we are at the harbor mouth.

Tony B. cuts the throttle.

The island is nearly underwater by now, but it is a comfort to remember that the tide will eventually turn.

Contributors

ELIZABETH ARNOLD is the congressional correspondent for National Public Radio. She made her way to Washington, D.C., after working for newspapers, wire services, and public radio in Alaska (in between commercial salmon seasons).

MALLORY BURTON has worked as a linguist and teacher on the northcoast of British Columbia for the past decade. Her serious and humorous fiction has appeared in numerous fly-fishing magazines and anthologies and will be published as a collection by Keokee Press in 1995.

LORIAN HEMINGWAY, half Cherokee Indian, was raised in the Deep South. Her many fishing pieces have appeared in the *New York Times, Sports Afield, America, Ocean Fantasy, Pacific Northwest* and *Horizon* magazines. Her novel, *Walking into the River*, (Simon and Schuster, 1993) was nominated for the Mississippi Institute of Arts and Letters Award for Fiction and has been published in eight countries.

PAM HOUSTON's collection of short stories, *Cowboys Are My Weakness* (W. W. Norton, 1993), was the winner of the 1993 Western States Book Award. She is the editor of *Women on Hunting* (Ecco, 1994), has published fiction in *Mirabella, Mademoiselle*, the *Mississippi Review*, and *Best American Short Stories;* and nonfiction in the *New York Times, Outside, House and Garden, Elle* and *Allure*. Houston is a licensed river guide and lives in Oakland, California, and Creede, Colorado.

GRETCHEN LEGLER is a creative writing professor at the University of Alaska at Anchorage. Her essay "Border Water," which appeared in *Uncommon Waters: Women Write About Fishing*

(Seal, 1991), won a Pushcart Prize. Her writing has appeared in several anthologies and her first book, *A Sportswoman's Notebook,* will be published in 1995 by Seal Press.

JESSICA MAXWELL is a columnist for *Audubon Magazine* and writes regularly for *Esquire* and numerous other publications. She is the author of *Salmon Circle* (HarperCollins, 1995) and is at work on a new book *The Last Best Fish: A Woman's Northwest Fly Fishing Adventure.* She lives in a cabin on an island in Washington's Puget Sound.

ALLISON MOIR is the associate editor of *Forbes FYI,* where she writes about sports, adventure travel, food and auctions. She lives in Manhattan but escapes to northern New England as often as possible.

JUDY MULLER is the daughter and granddaugher of fishing forebears. She began her journalistic career as a reporter for two newspapers in New Jersey. She switched to radio in 1977 and then from 1981 to 1990 was a news correspondent with CBS News in New York. In 1990 she moved to Los Angeles, where she is a television correspondent for ABC News, contributing reports to "World News Tonight with Peter Jennings," "Prime Time," "Good Morning, America" and "Nightline."

MARGOT PAGE is the editor of *The American Fly Fisher,* the quarterly journal of the American Museum of Fly Fishing, and the author of *Little Rivers: Tales of a Woman Angler* (Lyons & Burford, 1995). Her articles on fly fishing and other life matters have appeared in the *New York Times, Trout, Fly Rod & Reel, New Woman* and *American Health.* She and her husband, Tom Rosenbauer, live with their daughter, Brooke, not far from the Battenkill, in East Arlington, Vermont.

E. ANNIE PROULX won a Pulitzer Prize and the National Book Award for her novel *The Shipping News* (Scribner's, 1993; Touchstone, 1994). She is also the author of the novel *Postcards* (Scribner's, 1991) and the short story collection *Heart Songs and Other Stories* (Macmillan, 1994). She is an outdoorswoman and fly fisher and lives in Vermont.

LE ANNE SCHREIBER was born in Evanston, Illinois. She worked at *Time*, writing on foreign affairs, then covered the 1976 Olympics, and began a career in sports journalism, first becoming editor-in-chief of *WomenSports*, then editor of the *New York Times* sports section. In 1980 she left sports coverage to serve as the deputy editor of the *New York Times Book Review*, and four years later left New York City altogether to fish, tend to her garden and write. She is the author of *Midstream: The Story of a Mother's Death and a Daughter's Renewal* (Viking, 1990).

JENNIFER SMITH is a licensed Montana fishing outfitter and professional fly casting instructor. She has written for *Fly Rod & Reel, Fly Tackle Dealer, Scientific Anglers Guidebook* and other fly fishing publications. Jennifer has fished in Alaska, Florida, Canada, Argentina and Sweden. She is an instructor at the Dan Bailey Fly Fishing School in Livingston, Montana, and regularly holds casting clinics during the Federation of Fly Fishers' annual conclave.

SALLY I. STONER has closed a sixteen-year career as a pay check whore to pursue more exciting opportunities. She spends as much time as she can fly fishing and teaching other women about the sport. She lives in San Luis Obispo, California.

ELIZABETH STORER comes from a family of fishing enthusiasts, both men and women. With a background in film studies, her career took a twist when she moved from Los Angeles seven years ago and became a fly fishing guide. She has also worked as an environmental lobbyist and political activist. A writer and conservationist, outdoorswoman and pilot, she lives near Saratoga, Wyoming.

LIN SUTHERLAND is a an award-winning writer specializing in travel and humor. She has been published in *Field and Stream, Outdoor Photographer, Woman's Day* and numerous other magazines. She is a contributor to *Uncommon Waters: Women Write About Fishing* and *The Little Book of Fishing* (Grove Atlantic, 1994). She has just completed a collection of humorous memoirs about her unconventional family called *KinSHIP HAPPENS*. She is an adventure traveller and a horsewoman and lives on a ranch outside of Austin, Texas.

AILM TRAVLER lives in New Mexico where she writes, teaches and farms. She is a contributor to *Uncommon Waters: Women Write About Fishing* and *The Little Book of Fishing*.

JOAN SALVATO WULFF has written a fly casting column for *Fly Rod & Reel* since 1981 and has written for many other outdoor publications. She is the author of *Joan Wulff's Fly Casting Techniques* (Lyons & Burford, 1987) and *Joan Wulff's Fly Fishing: Expert Advice from a Woman's Perspective* (Stackpole, 1991). She lives in Lew Beach, New York, where she runs a nationally known fly-fishing school.

About the Editor

Holly Morris is the editor of *Uncommon Waters: Women Write About Fishing*, the first collection of women's fishing writing to be published. Originally from the Midwest, she fly fishes the Western states, works as an editor, and makes her home in Seattle.

Selected Sports and Outdoors Titles from Seal Press

UNCOMMON WATERS: *Women Write About Fishing,* edited by Holly Morris. $14.95, 1-878067-10-9. The bracing and meditative moments of fishing are captured in the words of thirty-four women anglers—from finessing trout and salmon in the Pacific Northwest to chasing bass and catfish in the Deep South.

ANOTHER WILDERNESS: *New Outdoor Writing by Women,* edited by Susan Fox Rogers. $14.95, 1-878067-54-0. Gutsy and inspirational, this collection of essays offers a range of experiences for the armchair adventurer—from snowboarding to deep sea diving.

WHEN WOMEN PLAYED HARDBALL by Susan E. Johnson. $14.95, 1-878067-43-5. A celebration of the brief yet remarkable era of the All-American Girls Professional Baseball League, filled with colorful stories and anecdotes by the ball players, play-by-play action, and insightful commentary.

LEADING OUT: *Women Climbers Reaching for the Top,* edited by Rachel da Silva. $16.95, 1-878067-20-6. Packed with riveting accounts of high peak ascents and narratives by some of the world's top climbers, this collection testifies to the power of discipline and desire.

THE CURVE OF TIME by M. Wylie Blanchet. $12.95, 1-878067-27-3. A fascinating true adventure story of a woman who packed her five children onto a twenty-five-foot boat and explored the coastal waters of the Pacific Northwest in the late 1920s.

WATER'S EDGE: *Women Who Push the Limits in Rowing, Kayaking and Canoeing* by Linda Lewis. $14.95, 1-878067-18-4. Ten candid profiles of women who have made their mark in these competitive sports—from pioneering rower Ernestine Bayer to long-distance canoer Valerie Fons.

Seal Press publishes many other books of fiction and non-fiction, including books on health, self-help and domestic violence, sports and outdoors, mysteries and women's studies. Order from us at 3131 Western Avenue, Suite 410, Seattle, Washington 98121. Please add 15% of the book total for shipping and handling. Write to us for a free catalog.